Quantity discounts are available. Please contact the publisher at the address below for details:

Lyons Den Press
P.O. Box 1341
Durham, North Carolina 27702

www.MapYourFinancialFuture.com

ISBN-13 978-0-9789488-0-1
ISBN-10 0-9789488-0-7
Printed in the United States of America

Map Your
Financial Freedom
Workbook

Charting a Course
Through Adulthood and Retirement

PATRICK A. LYONS

TABLE OF CONTENTS

This book is dedicated
to those who are struggling to
find financial freedom.

INTRODUCTION

Whether it involves paying bills, buying necessities or luxuries, saving for the future or holding a job, you deal with money on a daily basis. The information in this book is designed to complement *Map Your Financial Freedom: Charting a Course Through Adulthood and Retirement*, by providing worksheets and formulas to help make managing your finances much simple to deal with in this complex world in which we live.

This workbook is divided into four sections, which consist of nine lessons and short quizzes, to coincide with material covered in *Map Your Financial Freedom*.

Part 1 deals with the tools you need to get started on your financial journey, such as budgeting and establishing banking relationships. Part 2 explores the world of credit and identity theft. Part 3 examines education and how to start a business.

The final section of the book provides tools to build your investment portfolio so that, when the time comes, you can enjoy your retirement years. At the end of each section, you'll find a quick summary of the key points called "Things to Remember," discussion questions as well as some "Action Items" to get you firmly on your path to financial freedom.

PART 1

LESSON 1
BUDGETING

BUDGET OVERVIEW

Creating a budget is the foundation of a solid financial plan, and it is the first step you take toward achieving your financial goals. If you don't have a budget set up, there's no better time to start than now.

Part 1 of this workbook will teach you how to make budget. Put simply, a budget is a guide to help you live within your means. Because it requires that you track your income and expenses, some people believe that having such a plan means the end to fun. To the contrary, having a firm budget in place just means you have to put certain limits on your fun. Instead of going out every night of the week, for example, you can instead decide to go out twice a week and still stay within your budget.

Components of a Budget

Budgets consist of income and expenses. The expenses are broken down into fixed and variable costs:

> **Fixed costs** – These are expenses that remain the same each month. Examples of fixed costs include monthly payments for your car , insurance, or rent and/or mortgage payments.

> **Variable costs** – These amounts vary from month to month. Things such as utility and credit card bills would fall into the "variable costs" category.

Because most of your largest expenses will fall under "fixed costs," it is always best to try minimize these expenditures as much as possible to give you flexibility in dealing with changes in variable costs.

For example, natural gas prices (variable costs) more than doubled from 2003-2005, which caused heating bills to rise by a similar amount. In this case, you could adjust the home thermostat to potentially cut back on the cost, but it's a lot tougher to reduce your rent or mortgage payment. You could refinance a mortgage, but there are costs involved, and it's a much more complicated measure than simply turning down the thermostat. Moving is yet another option, but that process can possibly take months, and will nearly always cost you much more in the long term.

HOW TO SET UP A BUDGET

Take Advantage of Computer Programs

Microsoft Money and Quicken are the two leading personal finance software packages available to consumers. Each provides many of resources to help you better manage your personal finances, such as offering charts and graphs to monitor your spending. These programs can also help you set up debt-reduction and savings plans.

These software packages may also be used with online banking programs to assist in monitoring balances in your complete financial portfolio, such as checking, savings, money market, and investment accounts.

Money or Quicken is usually already installed on most computers. If not, you can purchase a basic version for about $30. There are more expensive versions that will assist in managing small businesses, but if you plan to manage just your household expenses, the standard version of either program will more than meet your needs

Manual Bookkeeping

If you don't have access to a personal finance software package or would prefer to use some other method of managing your money, tracking your budget with paper and pencil works just as well.

One of the best ways to set up a budget is to use a spending worksheet (see "Spending Worksheet Sample," below). Write down every thing you buy each day. Even if you purchase a postage stamp, record it. Being diligent about this will help set a reasonable guide for each expense category. For example, if your dining out expenses total $100 for the month and you are comfortable with that amount, then set that amount for your budget. If that is too much, then determine how much to cut.

NOTES

Spending Worksheet

Date	Description	Amount
4/1	McDonalds	$6.25
4/5	Mortgage	$900
4/10	Electric bill	$98
4/12	Cheesecake Factory	$49
4/14	Gas	$30
4/16	Life insurance	$50
4/20	Magazine subscription	$19
4/21	Gas	$30
4/24	Groceries	$121
4/26	Car payment	$385
4/27	Car insurance	$95

Total:
$1783.25

PITFALLS TO BUDGETING

Credit Cards – Holidays and vacations are when many of us resort to using credit. It's almost impossible to make travel plans without a credit card, and it's not uncommon to spend more on a trip than you planned, which will certainly cause a cash shortfall. Having to purchase gifts for several people during the holiday season can also cause you to go overboard.

Lack of adjustments – Budgets are not meant to be rigid; they should change over time. Since prices of goods and services rise over time, budgets should be adjusted at least once per year for inflation. Additionally, major events such as marriage or the birth of a child are other legitimate reasons to adjust your plan.

Impatience – If you are using a budget for the first time, it may take months before you develop a budget that strikes the perfect balance between your wants and needs. Give yourself time to adjust to this new way of working with money.

THINGS TO CONSIDER WHEN SETTING UP A BUDGET

Emergency Fund

The reality of life is that we have unexpected expenses, and they always seem to happen at the worst possible time. Your car just broke down, but you have to get to work so you can pay your bills. This is the kind of scenario that many of us can relate to, but how can we deal with these unforeseen costs without relying on credit cards? Creating an emergency fund can provide the cushion you need.

If you have an "emergency fund," you can withdraw from that account and not have to pull out a credit card to pay for unpredictable expenses. It's a good idea to work toward building a balance equal to four to six months of living expenses. You can achieve this goal by setting aside a small amount each pay period until you reach your target.

Fill in one of the budget worksheets at the end of this section to determine your monthly expenses. Multiply that number times five to determine your goal for your emergency fund. The fund should be invested in a money market or savings account because these pay more in interest than a typical checking account. It may take a couple of years to reach your goal, but once you get there you'll feel at ease knowing that you will be prepared when life's challenges occur.

	Emergency Fund Balance	**=**	Number of months needed (4-6)	**X**	Monthly Living Expenses

Splurge Fund

Some people feel that adhering to a budget is too restrictive. They want to "live a little" and go on shopping sprees, for example, out comes that handy credit card. But there is a solution that can help you abandon that mind-set: Set up a splurge fund.

Here's how it works: start a checking or money market account and make regular monthly deposits until you reach your proposed target. For example, if you want to have $600 to spend on a future shopping spree, you can deposit $100 a month into this fund until you reach that amount. Then, go to the mall and have fun – minus the guilt. You will leave the stores with a good feeling, knowing that you paid for your items with cash – not a high-interest credit card, which can take months or even years to pay off completely.

Gift Fund

Most of us don't think to include a section in our budgets to pay for gifts throughout the year, but it can keep you from racking up debt from Christmas and birthdays. To set up your gift fund, make a list of all the people for whom you purchase gifts during the year – and make sure to cover all "special occasions."

Next, assign a specific dollar amount for each occasion, and do not waver from that set figure. For example, for a sibling, you may choose to spend $25 for birthday gifts and $50 for Christmas presents. Next, take the total amount for all the gifts you plan to purchase for the year and divide by 12, which is the amount you will deposit into a savings account each month.

Setting up a gift fund can really help you avoid using credit cards, because as a birthday or special occasion approaches, you can withdraw from the account and not have to worry about paying a bill later.

GIFT FUND BUDGET
Use the table on the next page to set up your gift fund.

NOTES

Gift Fund Budget

	BIRTHDAY	HOLIDAY	SPECIAL OCCASION
Mother			
Father			
Grandparents			
Sibling 1			
Sibling 2			
Sibling 3			
Child 1			
Child 2			
Child 3			
Friend 1			
Friend 2			
Friend 3			
Other 1			
Other 2			
Other 3			
TOTAL			

Student Budget

INCOME	BUDGET	ACTUAL	ACTUAL – BUDGET
Wages			
Financial aid			
Miscellaneous			
Income Total			
EXPENSES			
Rent/Dorm			
Tuition			
Transportation			
Books			
Phone			
Dining out			
Entertainment			
Clothes			
Credit card			
Groceries/Meal Plan			
Expenses Total			
INCOME – EXPENSES			

Young Adult Budget

INCOME	BUDGET	ACTUAL	ACTUAL – BUDGET
Wages			
Miscellaneous			
Income Total			
FIXED EXPENSES			
Allowance			
Car Payment			
Rent/Mortgage			
Transportation			
Life Insurance			
Groceries			
Donations			
VARIABLE EXPENSES			
Utilities			
Dining Out			
Health Insurance			
Entertainment			
Loans/Credit Cards			
Gifts			
Investments/Savings			
Total Expenses			
INCOME – EXPENSES			

Blank Budget Form

	BUDGET AMOUNT	ACTUAL AMOUNT	BUDGET – ACTUAL
INCOME			
EXPENSES			
TOTAL EXPENSES			

Spending Worksheet

DATE	DESCRIPTION	AMOUNT
TOTAL		

Lesson 1 **QUIZ**

STOP

1. True or False: You should try to minimize variable costs.

2. Which of the following are pitfalls to budgeting?

a. credit cards
b. lack of adjustments
c. impatience
d. all of the above

3. True or False: An emergency fund should equal four to six months of living expenses.

4. A budget is a _____

a. Plan
b. Nightmare
c. Debt
d. Bad thing

5. Which of the following methods of tracking a budget was discussed earlier in this section?

a. Computer program
b. Memory
c. Manual
d. Both a & c

6. A gift fund is a way to _____ credit card usage.

a. Increase
b. Decrease
c. Maintain

LESSON 2
BANKING

BANKING OVERVIEW

Some people just don't trust banks with their money. Back in 1932 the stock market crashed and many banks went out of business, leading some former customers to keep their money under seat cushions and even mattresses for safer keeping.

However, things have changed a lot since those days. The Federal Deposit Insurance Corporation (FDIC) and the National Credit Union Association (NCUA) were each created to better protect account holders. So, if the bank goes out of business, you will still get your money back up to $250,000.

TYPES OF ACCOUNTS

Checking

There are two basic types of checking accounts: interest-bearing and non-interest bearing. In exchange for paying you interest on your money, interest-bearing accounts require a minimum balance. If your balance falls beneath that level, the financial institution will likely charge a monthly fee until your account returns to your bank's balance requirement.

Many banks are now also offering no-fee checking accounts; however in most cases, these accounts pay low or no interest on your balance. Because the amount paid on interest-bearing accounts usually is not that compelling, I encourage signing up for no-fee checking accounts.

Savings

Savings accounts mean just that: They encourage customers to keep money in their accounts. They offer a higher interest rate than checking accounts, withdrawals and deposits are allowed, but checks cannot be written against the balance in most cases.

Money Market

A money market account is another type of checking account. These accounts typically pay higher interest rates than basic checking accounts and require you to maintain a higher minimum balance.

BANKS VS. CREDIT UNIONS

Banks are for-profit institutions, meaning they have a vested interest in charging more for products to increase their earnings. Banks can have a national presence, like BankAmerica, or be more regional- or community-focused. They also tend to offer a wider array of loans and other products than credit unions.

Credit unions, on the other hand, are non-profit organizations, which tend to focus more on a particular area or community. These entities require a common bond such as working for a particular corporation.

Credit unions pay dividends (earnings paid out from its profits) to its members. The profits are also used to lower rates that members obtain on loans and increase returns they receive for deposits.

SHOPPING FOR THE BEST BANK

The table on the next page provides a checklist of questions to consider when shopping for a bank or credit union.

NOTES

_____

_____

_____

_____

_____

_____

_____

_____

_____

_____

Bank/Credit Union Evaluation

	BANK 1	BANK 2	BANK 3	BANK 4	BANK 5
Minimum balance	$100				
Monthly fees	$5				
Interest-bearing checking	No				
Savings account APR	4.5%				
Foreign ATM Fee	$3.50				
NSF Fee	$35				
Wire Transfer Fee	$30				
Online Banking	Yes				
Free online bill pay	No				
Convenience of branches	Yes				
Evening branch hours	No				
Weekend branch hours	No				
Direct deposit	Yes				
Offers credit cards	Yes				
Offers check cards	Yes				
FDIC or NCUA insured	Yes				

GLOSSARY OF BANK TERMS

Foreign ATM Fee – Fee charged for using an ATM other than ones owned by the financial institution in which you hold an account. Some banks do not charge foreign ATM fees, but others charge as much as $7 per transaction.

Monthly Fees – Some banks will charge fees if you don't maintain a minimum balance. Also, some financial institutions charge a per-check fee if you exceed their limit.

Non Sufficient Funds (NSF) Charge/Bounced Check Fee - When your account does not have enough funds to cover the cost of a check, your bank will charge a penalty, which can be $30 or more.

Online Banking – Online banking allows users to perform banking transactions on the Internet. You can transfer funds between accounts, view transactions and balances, stop payments on checks, and download transactions to personal finance programs, such as Microsoft Money or Quicken. The advantage of online banking is the ability to manage your money anywhere, anytime.

Online Bill Pay – This service permits users to pay bills on the Internet. Some online bill-pay services will send you email reminders to let you know a bill is due. These banks have incorporated encryption technology to prevent potential online hackers from getting their customers' account information.

Check Cards – These cards are used as a substitute for cash. Many retailers accept them, since they bear the Visa or MasterCard logo. However, no credit is involved. When a transaction is processed, the funds are automatically deducted from your checking account.

Depository Insurance – This is an instance in which financial institutions pay premiums to insure customer deposits. Banks and credit unions are insured by the Federal Deposit Insurance Corporation and the National Credit Union Association, respectively. Deposits are insured up to $250,000.

Bank/Credit Union Evaluation

	BANK 1	BANK 2	BANK 3	BANK 4	BANK 5
Minimum balance					
Monthly fees					
Interest-bearing checking					
Savings account APR					
Foreign ATM Fee					
NSF Fee					
Wire Transfer Fee					
Online Banking					
Free online bill pay					
Convenience of branches					
Evening branch hours					
Weekend branch hours					
Direct deposit					
Offers credit cards					
Offers check cards					
FDIC or NCUA insured					

STOP Lesson 2 **QUIZ**

1. **True or False:** A checking account usually pays more interest than a savings account.

2. **True or False:** A check card is a form of credit.

3. **Which type of account typically pays the highest interest on deposits?**
   a. No-fee checking
   b. Money market
   c. Interest-bearing checking

4. **True of False:** Banks require a common bond to open an account.

5. **The Federal Deposit Insurance Corporation insures member account holders' deposits up to:**
   a. $10,000
   b. $100
   c. $250,000

KEY

1. False. Savings accounts typically pay higher interest amounts than checking accounts to encourage account holders to save.

2. False. A check card is not a form of credit. When purchases are made using a check card, the amount is deducted from your checking account.

3. (b) Money market accounts pay higher interest amounts on deposits than checking accounts.

4. False. Credit unions require a common bond for membership. Some examples of bonds include family members or employers.

5. (c) The FDIC insures deposits at member banks up to $250,000 per account holder.

PART 1 REVIEW

Discussion Questions:

1. Write down a few financial goals (at least one short-term and long-term), and think of ways a budget can help achieve your objectives.

2. Ask family members and friends if they follow budgets. Find out some of the benefits/pitfalls they encounter.

3. What are some of the things that are important to you in choosing a bank or credit union?

ACTION ITEMS

	BEGIN DATE	COMPLETED
List monthly expenses		☐
Identify areas to cut spending		☐
Construct budget		☐
Start emergency fund		☐
Adjust budget		☐

NOTES

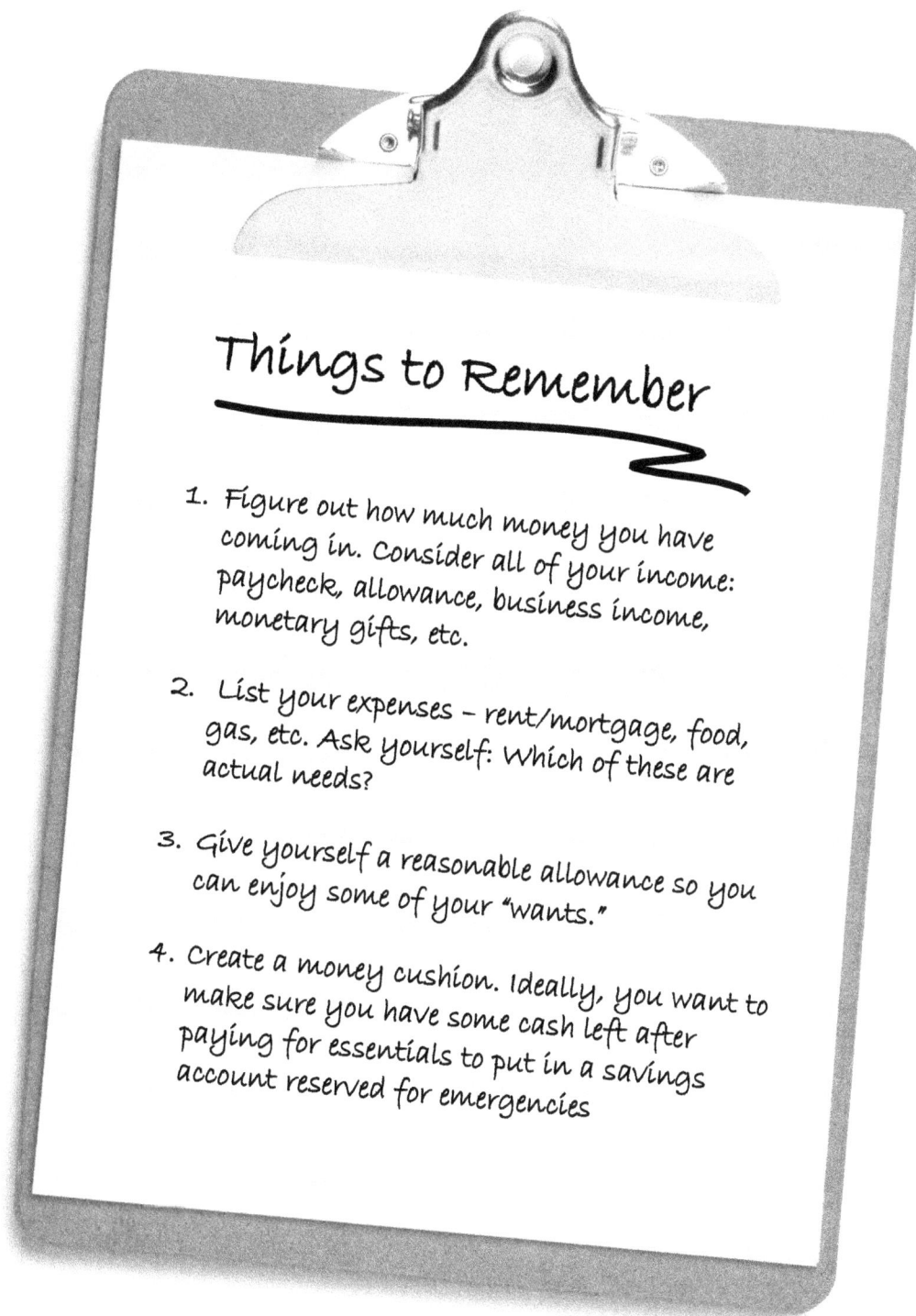

Things to Remember

1. Figure out how much money you have coming in. Consider all of your income: paycheck, allowance, business income, monetary gifts, etc.

2. List your expenses – rent/mortgage, food, gas, etc. Ask yourself: Which of these are actual needs?

3. Give yourself a reasonable allowance so you can enjoy some of your "wants."

4. Create a money cushion. Ideally, you want to make sure you have some cash left after paying for essentials to put in a savings account reserved for emergencies

END

END PART 1

PART 2

LESSON 3
CREDIT CARD BASICS

CREDIT OVERVIEW

Credit is needed for many things in today's economy, such as buying items on the Internet or reserving a hotel room. Part 2 of this workbook will explore ways of managing credit responsibly, while avoiding pitfalls that can set you back. It's important to remember that when you use a credit card, you are basically taking out a loan that must be repaid — with interest.

CREDIT CARD DEFINITIONS:

Annual Fee
A cost for the right to use the credit card

Annual Percentage Rate
The interest rate that is charged for borrowing,

Balance Transfer APR
Interest rate charged on balances transferred from other loans. Some lenders offer a teaser rate (low interest rate for a limited time), while others allow for a fixed rate until the balance transferred is paid in full.

Cash Advance APR
This is the interest rate charged for obtaining cash from a credit card. The rate is considerably higher than using regular credit transactions.

Compound Interest
Interest charged on top of interest. Interest is calculated on the total amount owed, which includes any unpaid principal and interest balances. Compounding interest is how credit card companies commonly compute interest charges.

Cure APR
If you have paid your bill on time for a continuous period, usually from 12 to 15 months, some lenders will reduce the APR from the default rate to a Cure rate, or your original APR.

Default APR

Interest rate that a lender charges to borrowers who do not uphold the initial loan terms. Lenders may, for example, increase your interest rate to the default rate if you make late payments on your balance.

Grace Period

The time period in which you can pay your balance in full to avoid interest charges. The typical grace period is 20-30 days, although some credit cards have no grace period.

Late Payment Fee

Fee charged for paying a bill late. This fee is in addition to your minimum monthly payment.

Method of Computing Balance

The monthly finance charge is computed by applying the monthly periodic rate to the average daily balance of credit transactions during the billing cycle.

Over-the-Credit Limit Fee

Fee charged if your balance exceeds your available credit limit. This fee is in addition to your monthly minimum payment.

Simple Interest

Interest grows at a stable rate based on a percentage of the principal balance. Simple interest is calculated only on the principal balance.

UNIVERSAL DEFAULT

According to the Internet site Wikipedia.com, universal default is a practice in the financial services industry whereby lenders can change the terms of a loan from normal to default when the lender is informed that the customer has defaulted on another lender.

Here's how it works, say you are paying your credit card bill on time, but happen to make a late payment on your car, the creditor can raise your interest rate to the default rate even though the two bills are not related. What's worse is that you may receive no advance warning of the increase in your APR.

The changes can also be retroactive, according to the Center For Responsible Lending. For instance, if the credit card company received word that your car payment was late in January, even if it is now June, you can be charged back interest on your credit card from the first date you were late with the car payment.

Credit card companies argue that they are justified in using Universal Default because all information available should be used in making credit decisions. A further rationale is that only raising the rates on delinquent customers allows better-paying customers the ability to enjoy lower rates because their rates are not affected.

TIPS TO PREVENT UNIVERSAL DEFAULT

> ➤ **Pay all bills on time.** Many banks offer free online bill payment. You can set up this service to help remind yourself when bills are due. Sometimes that little nudge is all we need to remember to pay bills in a timely manner.

> ➤ **Read the fine print.** It's important to read credit card disclosure statements to understand how the terms of your account can be changed. If you see wording such as, "We reserve the right to change the terms of this agreement at any time and for any reason," you have a card with universal default.

➢ **Transfer balances** to cards without universal default clauses

➢ **Don't overextend yourself with credit.** Try to keep your balances less than 50% of the available credit limit. Universal default can trigger default of other creditors if you are maintaining high credit balances.

➢ **Monitor credit reports regularly.** The major credit bureaus (such as Equifax) offer services that can provide updates on your credit report. If you plan to dispute a late payment, you will save yourself a lot of trouble if you do it right away.

CREDIT CARD EXERCISE

The following pages consist of sample credit card disclosure statements. You may receive these kinds of documents with a credit card offer. It is important to read the fine print and ask questions if you do not understand something. Carefully read each disclosure statement and complete the evaluation form that follows. Below is a brief description of each type of credit card offer:

➢ **Premium Home Equity Card** – This card offers credit based upon the equity in your home (difference between what is owed on your mortgage and the fair market value). Home equity credit cards are not like the typical home equity line of credit, which requires you to pledge your home as collateral in case you default. In this case, your available credit may be based on the equity in your home, but the APR will not be as low as a home equity line of credit because the lender cannot take your home if you default.

➢ **Easy Money Credit Card** – This is a "teaser rate" card, which offers 0% on balance transfers for a limited time period. Don't get suckered into teaser rate cards unless you plan to pay the balance before the rate goes up. Often, there are high fees to transfer balances. Also, make sure to read the "fine print" on these offers: Some companies will require you to maintain a certain balance after your transfer, or you will face penalties.

➢ **Jacked-Up Rewards Card** – This kind of card offers reward points for use of the credit card. If you travel a lot, a rewards card can be of value. Some programs give 5 frequent flyer miles for each dollar spent using the card. However, this type of card typically charges an annual fee, so make sure you will use it enough to justify the cost. Another tactic is to try to negotiate with the lender to have this charge waived.

➢ **Preferred Silver Card** – Preferred Silver cards are fixed-rate credit cards. Although you may be assigned a certain rate when you receive a card, again, it is possible to negotiate for a lower rate.

The Premium Home Equity Card
Very LOW FIXED rate!

Don't miss out on this opportunity to get the **Premium Home Equity Card NOW!**

BENEFITS

➤ Transfer high interest loans to a low fixed rate

➤ No Annual Fee

➤ Earn 2% cash back for all purchases

➤ Great Customer Service – Available 24/7

Important Information

Annual Percentage Rate (APR) for purchases and balance transfers	You will pay a finance charge of 7.75% for purchases
Other Annual Percentage Rates	Cash Advances: 23.50% Default APR: 29.75% Cure APR: 10.75%
Variable rate information	The APR for standard purchases may vary and is determined monthly by the Prime Rate (currently 7.75%). Your default rate may also vary and is determined by adding 22% to the Prime Rate.
Grace Period	1 day
Method of Computing Balances	Average daily balance (including new purchases)
Minimum Finance Charge	$1
Annual Fee	None
Miscellaneous Fees	Balance transfer fee: $10 Late payment fee: $10. Over-the-credit limit fee: $200 for each billing cycle balance is over credit limit Returned payment fee: $40

By applying for the Premium Home Equity card you authorize us to obtain credit reports to determine your initial credit limit and to make changes to your credit limit or terms. We may report our credit experience with others.

Default:: Your APR will be increased to the default rate if you have two or more late payments during a twelve-month period. We also reserve the right to demand full payment of any outstanding balances if you are in default.

Get rid of those high interest rate cards by consolidating them into one low payment.

Don't delay! This offer is only available for a limited time!

The EASY MONEY Credit Card

You are invited to apply for the
EASY MONEY CREDIT CARD!

BENEFITS

0% APR on balance transfers for 1 full year
No Annual Fee
Periodic reviews for credit limit increases
EASY Convenience Checks to consolidate bills
Customer Service you can depend on

Details of Rate, Fee and Other Cost Information	
Annual Percentage Rate (APR) for purchases and balance transfers	Upon approval a variable APR in the following range will be assigned to your account. 10.99% - 15.99%
Other Annual Percentage Rates	Cash Advances: 19.99% Balance Transfers: 0% until April 8, 2007, then the standard APR will be applied to all balances Delinquency APR: 19.99%
Variable rate information	The APR for standard purchases may vary and is determined monthly by adding an additional percentage amount to the Prime Rate based on your credit history.
Grace Period	None
Method of Computing Balances	Average daily balance (including new purchases)
Minimum Finance Charge	$2.50
Annual Fee*	$25. Annual fee is waived if you carry a balance greater than $2,500
Miscellaneous Fees	Balance transfer fee: $300 regardless of the transfer amount Convenience Check fee: $5 Minimum or 5% of the check amount ($200 maximum) Late payment fee: $50. Over-the-credit limit fee: $75 for each billing cycle balance is over credit limit by $500 Returned payment fee: $35

Default:: You will be in default if you: (1) fail to make any payment on time; (2) if you have provided inaccurate information on your application. If you pay your bill on time for twelve consecutive months following default, you account will be returned to the standard rate. We do not engage in the practice known as "Universal Default," which permits a credit card company to increase your APRs because you fail to make a payment on a loan with another lender or your credit history contains other negative information.

Save now by transferring your high rate balances!
You have nothing to lose!

JACKED UP Rewards Credit Card

You are cordially invited to apply for the Jacked Up Rewards Credit Card.

APPLY BEFORE JUNE 1, 2006,

and receive an added bonus – 15,000 miles after your first purchase!

BENEFITS

- Enjoy a credit limit up to $25,000
- Earn 2 miles for every $1 you spend
- Choose your reward: Cash, Gift Cards or Travel
- Fly anytime: No Blackout Dates
- Travel Accident Insurance – Automatic coverage up to $150,000
- Great Customer Service – Available 24/7

IMPORTANT INFORMATION

Annual Percentage Rate (APR) for purchases and balance transfers	Upon approval your account will be assigned one of the following rates: **11% for Platinum** **14% for Gold**
Other Annual Percentage Rates	Cash Advances: 24.50% Delinquency APR: 5 percentage points will be added to your APR for each late payment up to a maximum of 30%
Variable rate information	The APR for standard purchases may vary and is determined monthly by adding 3.25% or 6.25% to the Prime Rate (currently 7.75%); respectively for platinum and gold. Your default rate may also vary and is determined monthly as described above.
Grace Period	25 days. No grace period on cash advances
Method of Computing Balances	Two-cycle average daily balance (including new purchases)
Minimum Finance Charge	None
Annual Fee	$50 - Platinum Card $100 – Gold Card
Miscellaneous Fees	Balance transfer fee: 3% of each balance transfer, with a $25 minimum and $200 maximum Late payment fee: $15 for balances less than $1,000, $50 for balances greater than $1,000 Over-the-credit limit fee: $15 for each billing cycle balance is over credit limit Returned payment fee: $40 Replacement card fee: $25

We may change the rates, fees, and terms of your account at any time for any reason. These reasons may be based on information in your credit report, such as your failure to make payments to another creditor when due, amounts owed to: other creditors, the number of credit accounts outstanding, or the number of credit inquiries.

APPLY TODAY for this LIMITED-TIME offer!

The Preferred Silver Card

LOW FIXED RATE! You are pre-qualified for a
Preferred Silver Bank Credit Card with a limit up to $10,000!

BENEFITS

- **Low monthly payments**
- **No Annual Fee**
- **Fraud Protection provided at no charge**
- **Great Customer Service – Available 24/7**

IMPORTANT INFORMATION

Annual Percentage Rate (APR) for purchases and balance transfers	You will pay a finance charge of 0.032192% per day for purchases, which corresponds to an APR of 11.75%
Other Annual Percentage Rates	Cash Advances: 23.50% Default APR: 28.99% Cure APR: 21.99%
Variable rate information	The APR for standard purchases may vary and is determined monthly by adding 4% to the Prime Rate (currently 7.75%). Your default rate may also vary and is determined monthly as described above.
Grace Period	At least 25 days
Method of Computing Balances	Average daily balance (including new purchases)
Minimum Finance Charge	$1
Annual Fee	None
Miscellaneous Fees	Balance transfer fee: None Late payment fee: 10% of the minimum payment due. Over-the-credit limit fee: $35 for each billing cycle balance is over credit limit Returned payment fee: $20

By applying for the Preferred Silver card you authorize us to obtain credit reports in to determine your initial credit limit and to make changes to your credit limit or terms. We may report our credit experience with others.

Default: If you fail to make payments on time or if we in good faith reasonably believe that the prospect of payment to us or any other creditor is impaired, we reserve the right to increase your APR to the default rate. Preferred Silver Bank also reserves the right to demand full payment of your balance if you default.

Payment protection plan: Pays your credit card bill in the event of you become disabled, hospitalized or are laid off. The fee for this service is your total balance at the end of the billing period multiplied by $0.79 per $100. This fee is waived if you have paid for 84 consecutive months. This is a voluntary plan.

There's never been a better time to get the Preferred Silver Credit Card.

Apply online and receive APPROVAL IN 60 SECONDS!

Credit Card Disclosure Evaluation

TERMS	JACKED UP	PREFERRED SILVER	PREMIUM HOME EQUITY	EASY MONEY
What is the APR?				
Is there a teaser rate? If so, for how long?				
What is cash advance fee?				
What is default rate?				
Is there a cure rate?				
Is there a universal default clause?	Yes	Yes	No	No
Is there an annual fee? How much?				
Are there any balance transfer fees?				
Is there a grace period? If so, how long?				
What is the late payment fee?				
Is there an over-the-limit fee? How much?				
What is the best card? Why?				

The High, Hidden Cost of Default

It's very important to pay your credit card bills on time because most have clauses in their disclosure statements to increase interest rates if payment is received after the due date. Below is an example that illustrates how much interest you could pay by defaulting.

For this exercise, we will assign Credit Card A as the card that you initially received with a 13% APR. However, after being late in payment twice during the last 12 months, the credit card company raised your APR to the default rate of 26%.

The monthly payment in each scenario is the same — $25 for a $1,000 balance. As you can see from the table below, it will take more than four years to pay the bill, and it will cost you an additional $318 in interest costs (assuming you do not make any additional charges or incur any other fees).

If you are so unfortunate to default, the outcome is even worse: It will take 94 months (or, more than seven-and-a-half years) and cost you $1,350 in interest! This means you will pay a grand total of $2,350 to pay off your $1,000 credit card balance.

	INTEREST RATE	BALANCE	MONTHS TO PAY OFF	INTEREST COST
Credit Card A	13%	$1,000	53	$318
Default	26%	$1,000	94	$1,350

The table below highlights the costs if you double the monthly payment to $50 per month. As you can see, it will dramatically reduce your interest costs because more of the payment is going toward payment of the principal balance.

The moral of the story here is to pay more than the minimum payment whenever you possibly can. By doing so, you will pay off your debts faster, which increases your net worth!

	INTEREST RATE	BALANCE	MONTHS TO PAY OFF	INTEREST COST	SAVINGS
Credit Card A	13%	$1,000	23	$133	$185
Default	26%	$1,000	27	$325	$1,025

TYPES OF CREDIT TO AVOID

Payday Loans

Here's how payday loans work: You fill out an application, giving your contact information. You tell the company how much you want to borrow. (These companies typically lend up to $500.) Next, you give a post-dated check or authorization to debit your account. You then receive your cash, minus the fees (which range from $15-$30 per $100 borrowed). When payday comes, the lender cashes your check to satisfy the loan.

Sounds like that should be the end of the cycle, doesn't it? However, many people get caught in the debt trap and simply go back the next payday...and the next...and the next. The companies know this will likely happen, which is how they stay in business – essentially ripping you off.

Auto Title Loans

Auto title loans are short-term loans, typically 30 days or fewer. If you own your vehicle, you could use it to obtain this type of loan. Auto title loan companies couldn't care less if you have bad credit. To them, your car is your credit. If you don't pay the loan back, they are going to use the extra set of keys you provide when you apply for the loan to repossess your vehicle. The interest rate on the loan could be 30%, and that's just the rate for one month! So, if you have a $500 loan, the interest would be $150 ($500 * 30%). You would therefore owe $650 at the end of the month.

Refund Anticipation Loans (RALs)

Well, it's tax time again, and you want your refund fast, right? Tax preparation firms will be quick to offer you a refund anticipation loan (RAL). These companies essentially give you an advance against your refund, but it comes at a cost – and a steep one, at that.

Fees for the loan and preparation of tax forms can start at $100 and exceed $200 in some cases. If you make $10 per hour, that means you would have to work from 10 to 20 hours to make up the cost for the RAL. A better option, if you have Internet access is to use an online tax preparation company. Many are part of the IRS's Free File program, which allows consumers to file their tax returns electronically for free if you meet certain requirements. Check http://www.irs.gov for more details. In many cases, you can receive your tax refund within two weeks of filing electronically. So it's really best to be patient — and receive all of your refund.

Overdraft Loans

Most of us have written a bad check at some point in our lives. However, be wary of overdraft loans that financial institutions offer to cover bounced checks. Why? Because these programs are not in business to do you any favors. You will still be charged fees for insufficient funds if you write a bad check with this type of loan, which can range from $20-$35, according to the Center for Responsible Lending.

You will also pay interest charges on the loan. When your next deposit is made, your bank will deduct its fees, and the remainder will be available to you. Instead of signing up for an overdraft loan see if your financial institution will allow you to use a savings account or money market account for overdraft purposes. You will still be charged a fee for not having the funds to cover the bounced check, but you will avoid paying your bank extra interest for an overdraft loan. Also, the funds to cover the check will be deducted from the account you designate as opposed to paying the interest charges and other fees banks charge for overdraft loans.

Fee Comparison

The table below compares the fees you would incur from paying bills late to those for taking out a high cost loan. As you can see, you are better off paying your bill late than using payday loans, auto title refund anticipation loans, and overdraft loans.

TRANSACTIONS	FEES/MONTH	APR
$205 payday loan	$77	457%
$205 bounced check	$43	255%
$80 overdraft loan repaid in 2 weeks	$22.50	733%
Late fee on $205 credit card bill	$30	178%
Late fee on $800 mortgage	$32	48%
Late fee on $600 rent payment	$30	60%
Late fee on $300 car payment	$15	60%
$500 Auto title loan	$150	360%
Source: Center for Responsible Lending		

Here are some tips from the Consumer Federation of America on how to best handle cash crunches without borrowing:

➢ Before you are late on a rent, mortgage, or utility payment, speak with the creditor. For non-interest bills, such as utility or telephone bills, inquire about making payment arrangements. Make sure to ask about fees or extra costs for extended payments.

➢ Delay the purchase of expensive items until you have cash. In this case, you really should do all you can: For example, even if a car repair is causing a cash-flow problem, explore public transportation options until you have the funds – in cash — to repair your vehicle.

➢ Apply for assistance programs, such as emergency utility funds. Take advantage of local charity, religious, or community programs that help families make ends meet in a crisis.

➢ Work overtime or pick up extra work to bring in more income. Sell items of value that you no longer need.

➢ Consider adjusting the amount withheld for taxes to provide more money in your paycheck instead of over-withholding every payday to get a big tax refund later.

STOP

Lesson 3 **QUIZ**

1. **True or False:** The over-the-limit fee is in addition to your monthly payment.

2. **Which method of computing interest charges interest on top of interest?**
   a. Simple
   b. Compound
   c. Fixed

3. **True or False:** Paying more than the monthly minimum payment will cause you to pay less in interest charges.

4. **Credit card companies engaging in the practice of universal default will ___ your APR for late payments to other creditors.**
   a. Decrease
   b. Not change
   c. Increase

5. **Which of the following is the best source of cash in case of an emergency?**
   a. Payday loan
   b. Refund anticipation loan
   c. Overdraft loan
   d. Auto title loan
   e. None of the above

KEY

1. True. If your monthly payment is $25 and your credit card company charges an over-the-limit fee of $35, you will be required to pay $60 ($25 + $35) when the bill is due.

2. (b) Compounding interest charges interest on top of interest

3. True. Monthly payments are set to amounts that range from 2%–4% of your balance. If you have a high APR, a large portion of your payment will be used to pay interest charges.

4. (c) If you are late with your mortgage, your credit card company can increase your APR if it has a universal default clause in its disclosure statement.

5. (e) None of these choices are good ones. Try your best to establish an emergency fund to assist in cash crunches.

LESSON 4
UNDERSTANDING CREDIT REPORTS
& STRATEGIES FOR IMPROVING CREDIT SCORES

OVERVIEW

The choices you make today will affect you in the future. That's why it's important to use credit wisely, because any missteps will stay on your credit report for several years, as the chart below indicates:

OPEN ACCOUNT IN GOOD STANDING	INDEFINITELY
Late or missed payment	7 years
Collection accounts	7 years
Chapter 7 bankruptcy	10 years
Chapter 13 bankruptcy	7 years
Unpaid tax liens	15 years
Paid tax lien	7 years
Credit inquiries	2 years

Source: Experian

SECTIONS OF CREDIT REPORTS

Although each of the major credit reporting companies, Equifax, Experian, and TransUnion, have their own credit reports, they all have a similar structure - sections for personal information, account information, public records and inquiries. Let explore each part.

Personal Information

This section basically lists information that identifies you. It would include such items as your name, social security number, and address.

Account Information

This section lists all credit accounts in your name, such as installment loans, like car payments, or revolving credit, like credit cards. Your account balance and available credit is noted in this section as well. Each credit bureau has its own way of marking payments to your account, whether on time or late.

Public Records

The public records section includes information that comes from court documents, such as bankruptcy filings or unpaid tax liens.

Inquiries

There are two types of inquiries - those initiated by you and those opened by creditors. If you apply for a new loan, any inquiries you've made would show up on your list. The other type of inquiry could occur if a credit card company views your credit report to decide whether to offer you a new card or loan.

HOW AND WHERE TO GET YOUR CREDIT REPORT:

Equifax	(800) 685-1111	www.equifax.com
Experian	(888) 397-3742	www.experian.com
TransUnion	(800) 888-4213	www.transunion.com

You can also order credit reports from all three credit reporting companies by visiting www.annualcreditreport.com or calling **(877) 322-8228.**

---

experian®

Online Personal Credit Report from Experian for

Experian credit report prepared for **JOHN Q CONSUMER** Your report number is **1562064065** Report date: **01/24/2005**	Index: - Potentially negative items - Accounts in good standing - Requests for your credit history - Personal information - Important message from Experian - Contact us

Experian collects and organizes information about you and your credit history from public records, your creditors and other reliable sources. Experian makes your credit history available to your current and prospective creditors, employers and others as allowed by law, which can expedite your ability to obtain credit and can make offers of credit available to you. We do not grant or deny credit; each credit grantor makes that decision based on its own guidelines.

Potentially Negative Items

back to top

Public Records

Credit grantors may carefully review the items listed below when they check your credit history. Please note that the account information connected with some public records, such as bankruptcy, also may appear with your credit items listed later in this report.

MAIN COUNTY CLERK

Address: 123 MAINTOWN S BUFFALO , NY 10000	Identification Number: 1	Plaintiff: ANY COMMISSIONER O.
Status: Civil claim paid.		Status Details: This item was verified and updated on 06-2001.

Date Filed: 10/15/2000	Claim Amount: $200
Date Resolved: 01/04/2001	Liability
Responsibility: INDIVIDUAL	Amount: NA

Credit Items

For your protection, the last few digits of your account numbers do not display.

ABCD BANKS

Address: 100 CENTER RD BUFFALO, NY 10000 (555) 555-5555	Account Number: 1000000....
Status: Paid/Past due 60 days.	

Date Opened: 10/1997	Type: Installment	Credit Limit/Original Amount: $523
Reported Since: 11/1997	Terms: 12 Months	High Balance: NA
Date of Status: 01/1999	Monthly Payment: $0	Recent Balance: $0 as of 01/1999 Recent Payment: $0
Last Reported: 01/1999	Responsibility: Individual	

Account History:
60 days as of 12-1998
30 days as of 11-1998

Report number:

You will need your report number to contact Experian online, by phone or by mail.

Index:

Navigate through the sections of your credit report using these links.

Potentially negative items:

Items that creditors may view less favorably. It includes the creditor's name and address, your account number (shortened for security), account status, type and terms of the account and any other information reported to Experian by the creditor. Also includes any bankruptcy, lien and judgment information obtained directly from the courts.

Status:

Indicates the current status of the account.

If you believe information in your report is inaccurate, you can dispute that item quickly, effectively and cost free by using Experian's online dispute service located at:

www.experian.com/disputes

Disputing online is the fastest way to address any concern you may have about the information in your credit report.

Sample Credit Report

MAIN COLL AGENCIES

Address:	Account Number:	Original Creditor:
PO BOX 123	0123456789	TELEVISE CABLE COMM.
ANYTOWN, PA 10000		
(555) 555-5555		

Status: Collection account. $95 past due as of 4-2000.

Date Opened:	Type:	Credit Limit/Original Amount:
01/2000	Installment	$95
Reported Since:	Terms:	High Balance:
04/2000	NA	NA
Date of Status:	Monthly	Recent Balance:
04/2000	Payment:	$95 as of 04/2000
	$0	Recent Payment:
Last Reported:	Responsibility:	$0
04/2000	Individual	

Your statement: ITEM DISPUTED BY CONSUMER

Account History:
Collection as of 4-2000

back to top

Accounts in Good Standing 5

AUTOMOBILE AUTO FINANCE

Address:	Account Number:
100 MAIN ST E	12345678998....
SMALLTOWN, MD 90001	
(555) 555-5555	

Status: Open/Never late.

Date Opened:	Type: 6	Credit Limit/Original Amount:
01/2000	Installment	$10.355
Reported Since:	Terms:	High Balance:
01/2000	65 Months	NA
Date of Status:	Monthly	Recent Balance:
08/2001	Payment:	$7,984 as of 08/2001
	$210	Recent Payment:
Last Reported:	Responsibility:	$0
08/2001	Individual	

MAIN

Address:	Account Number:
PO BOX 1234	1234567899876
FORT LAUDERDALE, FL 10009	

Status: Closed/Never late.

Date Opened:	Type:	Credit Limit/Original Amount:
03/1991	Revolving	NA
Reported Since:	Terms:	High Balance:
03/1991	1 Months	$3,228
Date of Status:	Monthly	Recent Balance:
08/2000	Payment:	$0 /paid as of 08/2000
	$0	Recent Payment:
Last Reported:	Responsibility:	$0
08/2000	Individual	

Your statement:
Account closed at consumer's request

Accounts in good standing:

Lists accounts that have a positive status and may be viewed favorably by creditors. Some creditors do not report to us, so some of your accounts may not be listed.

Type:

Account type indicates whether your account is a revolving or an installment account.

Requests for Your Credit History `7`

back to top

Requests Viewed By Others

We make your credit history available to your current and prospective creditors and employers as allowed by law. Personal data about you may be made available to companies whose products and services may interest you.

The section below lists all who have requested in the recent past to review your credit history as a result of actions involving you, such as the completion of a credit application or the transfer of an account to a collection agency, mortgage or loan application, etc. Creditors may view these requests when evaluating your creditworthiness.

HOMESALE REALTY CO

Address:	Date of Request:
2000 S MAINROAD BLVD STE	07/16/2001
ANYTOWN CA 11111	
(555) 555-5555	

Comments:
Real estate loan on behalf of 1000 COPRORATE COMPANY. This inquiry is scheduled to continue on record until 8-2003.

ABC BANK

Address:	Date of Request:
PO BOX 100	02/23/2001
BUFFALO NY 10000	
(555) 555-5555	

Comments:
Permissible purpose. This inquiry is scheduled to continue on record until 3-2003.

ANYTOWN FUNDING INC

Address:	Date of Request:
100 W MAIN AVE STE 100	07/25/2000
INTOWN CA 10000	
(555) 555-5555	

Comments:
Permissible purpose. This inquiry is scheduled to continue on record until 8-2002.

Requests Viewed Only By You

The section below lists all who have a permissible purpose by law and have requested in the recent past to review your information. You may not have initiated these requests, so you may not recognize each source. We offer information about you to those with a permissible purpose, for example, to:

- other creditors who want to offer you preapproved credit;
- an employer who wishes to extend an offer of employment;
- a potential investor in assessing the risk of a current obligation;
- Experian or other credit reporting agencies to process a report for you;
- your existing creditors to monitor your credit activity (date listed may reflect only the most recent request).

We report these requests **only to you** as a record of activities. We **do not** provide this information to other creditors who evaluate your creditworthiness.

MAIN BANK USA

Address:	Date of Request:
1 MAIN CTR AA 11	08/10/2001
BUFFALO NY 10000	

MAINTOWN BANK

Address:	Date of Request:
PO BOX 100	08/05/2001
MAINTOWNS DE 10000	
(555) 555-5555	

ANYTOWN DATA CORPS

Address:	Date of Request:
2000 S MAINTOWN BLVD STE	07/16/2001
INTOWN CO 11111	
(555) 555-5555	

Requests for your credit history:

Also called "inquiries", requests for your credit history are logged on your report whenever anyone reviews your credit information. There are two types of inquiries.

Requests viewed by others

Inquiries resulting from a transaction initiated by you. These include inquiries from your applications for credit, housing or other loans. They also include transfer of an account to a collection agency. Creditors may view these items when evaluating your creditworthiness.

Requests viewed only by you

Inquiries resulting from transactions you may not have initiated but that are allowed under the FCRA. These include preapproved offers, as well as for employment, investment review, account monitoring by existing creditors, and requests by you for your own report. These items are shown only to you and have no impact on your creditworthiness or risk scores.

Personal Information 　8

The following information is reported to us by you, your creditors and other sources. Each source may report your personal information differently, which may result in variations of your name, address, Social Security number, etc. As part of our fraud-prevention program, a notice with additional information may appear. As a security precaution, the Social Security number that you used to obtain this report is not displayed. The Geographical Code shown with each address identifies the state, county, census tract, block group and Metropolitan Statistical Area associated with each address.

Names:
JOHN Q CONSUMER
JONATHON Q CONSUMER
J Q CONSUMER

Social Security number variations:
999999999

Year of birth:
1954

Employers:
ABCDE ENGINEERING CORP

Telephone numbers:
(555) 555 5555 Residential

Address: 123 MAIN STREET
ANYTOWN, MD 90001-9999
Type of Residence: Multifamily
Geographical Code: 0-156510-31-8840　9

Address: 555 SIMPLE PLACE
ANYTOWN, MD 90002-7777
Type of Residence: Single family
Geographical Code: 0-176510-33-8840

Address: 999 HIGH DRIVE APT 15B
ANYTOWN, MD 90003-5555
Type of Residence: Apartment complex
Geographical Code: 0-156510-31-8840

Personal information:

Personal information associated with your history that has been reported to Experian by you, your creditors and other sources.

May include name and Social Security number variations, employers, telephone numbers, etc. Experian lists all variations so you know what is being reported to us as belonging to you.

Address information:

Your current address and previous address(es)

Your Personal Statement 　10

No general personal statements appear on your report.

Personal statement:

Any personal statement that you added to your report appears here.

Important Message From Experian　back to top

By law, we cannot disclose certain medical information (relating to physical, mental, or behavioral health or condition). Although we do not generally collect such information, it could appear in the name of a data furnisher (i.e., "Cancer Center") that reports your payment history to us. If so, those names display in your report, but in reports to others they display only as MEDICAL PAYMENT DATA. Consumer statements included on your report at your request that contain medical information are disclosed to others.

Note - statements remain as part of the report for 2 years and display to anyone who has permission to review your report.

Contacting Us　back to top

Contact address and phone number for your area will display here.

CREDIT SCORES

According to Wikipedia.com, a credit score is a credit rating that represents an estimate of an individual's financial creditworthiness as calculated by a statistical model.

The score is computed using information from your credit report. It does not include data such as your race or marital status. FICO (owned by Fair Isaac Corporation) has the most popular scoring model, but each of the major credit reporting companies has its own.

Scores generally range from 300 - 850. A score of 700 or higher is considered good, while scores in the 500s are weak. Credit scores can directly affect your ability to receive a loan, and these scores will also affect your interest rate — if you are approved.

For example, someone with a score of 550 may get approved for a credit card, but will likely receive a higher interest rate than someone with a higher (better) score. It's important not to get caught up so much in your actual score as it is to focus on the factors that affect the number:

1.　**Payment history** – Late payments will affect your score more than any other factor. All late payments are bad, but one that occurred last month will affect you more than the one that transpired five years ago.

STRATEGIES FOR PAYING DOWN DEBTS

One of the first things I suggest is to take an inventory of your debts. (For your convenience, you can use the table provided below).

If you have small debts, definitely pay them off first. They can be eliminated more quickly, and it will give you a strong sense of accomplishment when you eliminate a bill. The funds used to reduce the small debts can then be applied to larger ones. So, the rule of thumb should be, after the small ones are gone, attack the ones with the highest interest rates next.

CREDIT CARDS

NAME	INTEREST RATE	MONTHLY PAYMENT	CURRENT BALANCE

OTHER DEBTS (Mortgage, Automobile, Business, School)

NAME	INTEREST RATE	MONTHLY PAYMENT	CURRENT BALANCE

2. **Utilization or balance-to-limit ratio** – Try to keep your credit balance less than 30% of your total available credit. Here's an example: If you have $10,000 in available credit among three cards, keep your balance less than $3,000. High credit usage (30% or greater) suggests you could overextend yourself, which may impact your ability to pay your bills.

3. **Types of Accounts** – Lenders like to see that people can handle different types of credit (installment, revolving, etc.) and pay the bills on time because it shows you know how to manage your credit responsibly.

4. **Inquiries** – Opening several new credit accounts within a short time period can lower your score. However, inquiries have the smallest impact on credit scores.

CREDIT REPAIR SCAMS

I'm sure you've heard commercials on the radio or television that promise to wipe bad debts from your credit report. Don't fall for these scams! You can do anything these credit repair companies can do. You can call to renegotiate payment terms if you become overextended with debt payments; you can go to a credit counselor for assistance. To find a reputable credit counselor close to you, check the National Foundation for Credit Counseling (www.nfcc.org).

Handling Disputes

It's a good idea to check your credit report at least twice a year to ensure there are no errors. By law you are entitled to receive one free report annually.

In addition, the major credit reporting companies each sell products that monitor credit reports on a more frequent basis and will report any unusual activity to you, if and when it occurs.

NOTES

SAMPLE DISPUTE LETTER:

Dear Sir or Madam:

I recently received a copy of my credit report and discovered that it contains inaccurate information.

Account XYZ: This is not my account.
Account ABC: I have never been late on this account.

My full name is: John Smith

My Social Security Number is: 123-45-XXXX

My date of birth is: April 1, 1987

My address is: 57 Swordfish Lane, Anywhere, FL 32450

Please investigate this matter, correct and delete the inaccurate information from my credit file, and send me an updated credit report.

If you have any questions, feel free to give me a call at (XXX) 867-5309 or email me at info@patrickalyons.com.

Thank you for your attention to this matter.

Sincerely,

John Smith

John Smith

Charge Offs

A charge off occurs if a bill has not been paid in four months. For bookkeeping purposes, the creditor "writes off" the debt, but that doesn't get you off the hook. You still owe the debt. At this point a collection agency may purchase the debt from the credit card company and make efforts to get you to pay the bill.

Sometimes, collection agencies will offer a settlement for the balance. In most cases, expect to pay at least 50% of the balance to have it settled. In return, try to negotiate to have the debt deleted from your credit report when you make or receive a settlement offer. Some bill collectors will balk, but it never hurts to ask. Also make sure you have a signed letter from someone who is authorized to accept a resolution before sending any money.

NOTES

SAMPLE SETTLEMENT LETTER:

Dear Sir or Madam:

According to my credit report, I owe $500 for account # 987654321.

I am writing to inquire if you will accept my offer of $300 to satisfy the account as paid in full. I am requesting that by accepting this offer, your company will notify Equifax, Experian, and TransUnion to delete this account from my files upon receiving my payment. I will send a certified check within 10 business days of your acceptance of this offer.

If you have any questions, feel free to give me a call at (XXX) 867-5309 or email me at info@patrickalyons.com.

Thank you for your attention to this matter.

Sincerely,

John Smith

John Smith

STOP

Lesson 4 QUIZ

1. **How many years will an unpaid tax lien remain on your credit report?**

   a. 1
   b. 7
   c. 15

2. **The personal information section of a credit report includes:**

   a. Name
   b. Income
   c. Shoe size
   d. All of the above

3. **True or False:** Credit repair companies are a great way to rebuild your credit history.

4. **True or False:** A charge off is a term used to describe a debt that has not been paid in four months.

5. **What factor affects credit scores the most?**

   a. Types of accounts
   b. Income
   c. Payment history

KEY

1. (c) Unpaid tax liens remain on credit reports for 15 years.

2. (a) Your name would appear in the personal information section of a credit report. Other information in the section could include your address and social security number.

3. False. You can do anything a credit repair company can do

4. True. Accounts become "charge offs," or collection accounts, if a bill is four months late.

5. (c) Payment history affects credit scores more than any other factor.

LESSON 5
AVOIDING IDENTITY THEFT

OVERVIEW

If you've been paying attention to the news lately, you'll know that identity theft is costing consumers and corporations billions of dollars in losses. There are two main categories for identity theft: criminal and financial. Criminal theft occurs when someone assumes your identity with the intent of committing crimes. Financial theft, which we will focus on here, is when a thief acquires your account information with the intent of stealing your financial assets.

IMPORTANT NUMBER INVENTORY

Use the table below to list important identification numbers and store in a secure location. This information will be useful in the event you ever lose your wallet or someone steals your purse. *Do not share this information with anyone.*

Important Number Inventory:

	ACCOUNT NUMBER	PASSWORD
Social Security		
Driver's license		
Life Insurance		
ATM card		
Checking account		
Cell phone		
Credit card		
Credit card		

HOW IDENTITY THEFT CAN OCCUR

Phishing Emails – These are emails that are "phishing" for your information on the Internet. Often, thieves will send emails claiming to be a financial institution, such as a bank or credit card company. There may be an urgent appeal to click on a link that directs you to a website that will ask for your personal information. Avoid clicking on links within emails even if you believe it is from a legitimate source. If you receive an email from someone claiming to be XYZ Corporation, go directly to that website to ensure it is a credible, legitimate company to prevent giving personal information to scammers.

SAMPLE PHISHING EMAILS: SAMPLE 1

Home   Profile   People   Mail   Photos   More ▾

New   Delete   Junk   Mark as ▾   Move to ▾   🖶 POP

Reply   Reply all   Forward   ⬇ ⬆

Security Update

From: **John Smith**

Sent: **Mon 11/18/2009 9:15 AM**

To: **info@PatrickALyons.com**

Big Great Bank

Valued Big Great Bank Client

In our bank, we value our clients and money; that's why we have to upgrade our database. The upgrade requires our customers to update their debit/credit card information to avoid problems in our ATM services.

Click here to update your information.

Sincerely,

CEO, Big Great Bank

Reply   Reply all   Forward   Delete   POP   ⬇ ⬆

SAMPLE PHISHING EMAILS: SAMPLE 2

Home   Profile   People   Mail   Photos   More ▾

New   Delete   Junk   Mark as ▾   Move to ▾   🖶   POP

Reply   Reply all   Forward   ⬇⬆

Valued Client

From: **John Smith**

Sent: **Tues 11/19/2009 1:32 PM**

To: **info@PatrickALyons.com**

The One and Only Credit Company

Dear Client,

It has come to our attention that your billing information is out of date. This requires you to take 5-10 minutes to update your information on our secure website to prevent any future problems with your account. However, failure to update your records will result in account termination. Please update your account within the next 24 hours to avoid any interruptions in your account. Failure to do so will result in cancellation of service, Terms of Service (TOS) violations or future billing problems.

Please click here to update your billing records.

Sincerely,

Sr. Vice President, Billing Department
The One and Only Credit Card Company

Reply   Reply all   Forward   Delete   POP   ⬇⬆

OTHER FORMS OF FRAUDULENT ACTIVITY:

Phone – There have been instances where people have received calls from individuals claiming to work for credit card companies. These scammers will attempt to get you to share the 3-digit security code on the back of your credit card. This code was designed expressly for your own protection when completing transactions where you aren't present, such as on the Internet or phone. Don't fall for this scam. Only share account information on the phone with sources you trust. To reduce calls from telemarketers, sign up for the Do Not Call Directory (www.donotcall.gov).

Trash – It's not uncommon for pilferers to look through your trash to get account numbers and other personal information. Instead of just throwing those pre-approved credit card offers away, be sure to shred them and any other sensitive documents with a cross-shredder to prevent thieves from reconstructing them.

Business Records – Scam artists can hack into corporate databases to steal sensitive information. Check with your employer to see what type of protection they have in place (such as Firewall software) to prevent others from viewing your personal information.

Mailboxes – Did you know that a lot of identity theft occurs from your own mailbox? You can prevent this by using online bill-pay services or going directly to the post office to deposit sensitive information.

Stealing Directly From You – In many cases, individuals will steal your purse or wallet to get access to your credit cards or checks. To prevent this, men should carry wallets in their side pockets instead of back pockets. Women should avoid carrying backpack-type purses because thieves can potentially access them without your knowledge.

TIPS FOR AVOIDING IDENTITY THEFT

➢ Never share passwords with anyone. Also, don't use common IDs, such as birthdays or family member names for passwords.

➢ Don't carry your social security card or passwords in your wallet. Only carry the identification you will need on a daily basis. If you have multiple credit cards but only use one, store the others in a secure location in your home.

➢ Never leave ATM receipts at the ATM. Take them home and shred them immediately.

➢ Check your credit reports at least twice a year for unusual account activity.

➢ Be aware of your surroundings when you are at ATMs. If possible, avoid using them at night, because your vision is limited, and there are fewer passersby to either witness or even thwart an attempt to take your ATM card.

ADDITIONAL IDENTITY THEFT RESOURCES

Hoax-Slayer (http://www.hoax-slayer.com/) **and Anti-Phishing Working Group** – (http://www.antiphishing.org/). These are very good sources for phishing email examples and information on other Internet scams.

Federal Trade Commission – (http://www.ftc.gov/bcp/edu/microsites/idtheft) – The FTC website offers tips on preventing identity theft and the steps to take if you do become a victim.

Lesson 5 **QUIZ**

STOP

1. **True or False:** It's OK to share your passwords with friends.

2. **Which of the following is a good way to prevent identity theft?**
   a. Not shredding credit card receipts.
   b. Storing sensitive documents in a safe.
   c. Clicking on links within emails.

3. **What type of information might a phisher try to acquire from you?**

   a. Shoe size
   b. Favorite recipe
   c. Credit card account number

4. **To prevent thieves from stealing from your mailbox, what should you do?**
   a. Mail important letters at the post office.
   b. Have bills and sensitive documents mailed to a P.O. box.
   c. Both a & b.

KEY

1. False. Don't share passwords with anyone, because even friends and family members commit a lot of identity theft.

2. (b) Storing sensitive documents in a safe or lockbox in a location that only you are aware of is a good way to reduce the risk of identity theft.

3. (c) Phishers are interested in getting account information so they can steal from you.

4. (c) Both a & b are ways of preventing thieves from stealing personal information from your mail.

PART 2 REVIEW

Discussion Questions:

1. **What are some things you can do to prevent Universal default?**

2. **How can having a poor credit history hurt you in the real world?**

3. **What are some ways to prevent identity theft that weren't discussed in this workbook?**

ACTION ITEMS

	BEGIN DATE	COMPLETED
Pay more than minimum payment on credit accounts		☐
Order copy of credit report		☐
Negotiate with creditors for lower interest rates		☐
Purchase a cross-shredder		☐

NOTES

_____

_____

_____

_____

_____

_____

_____

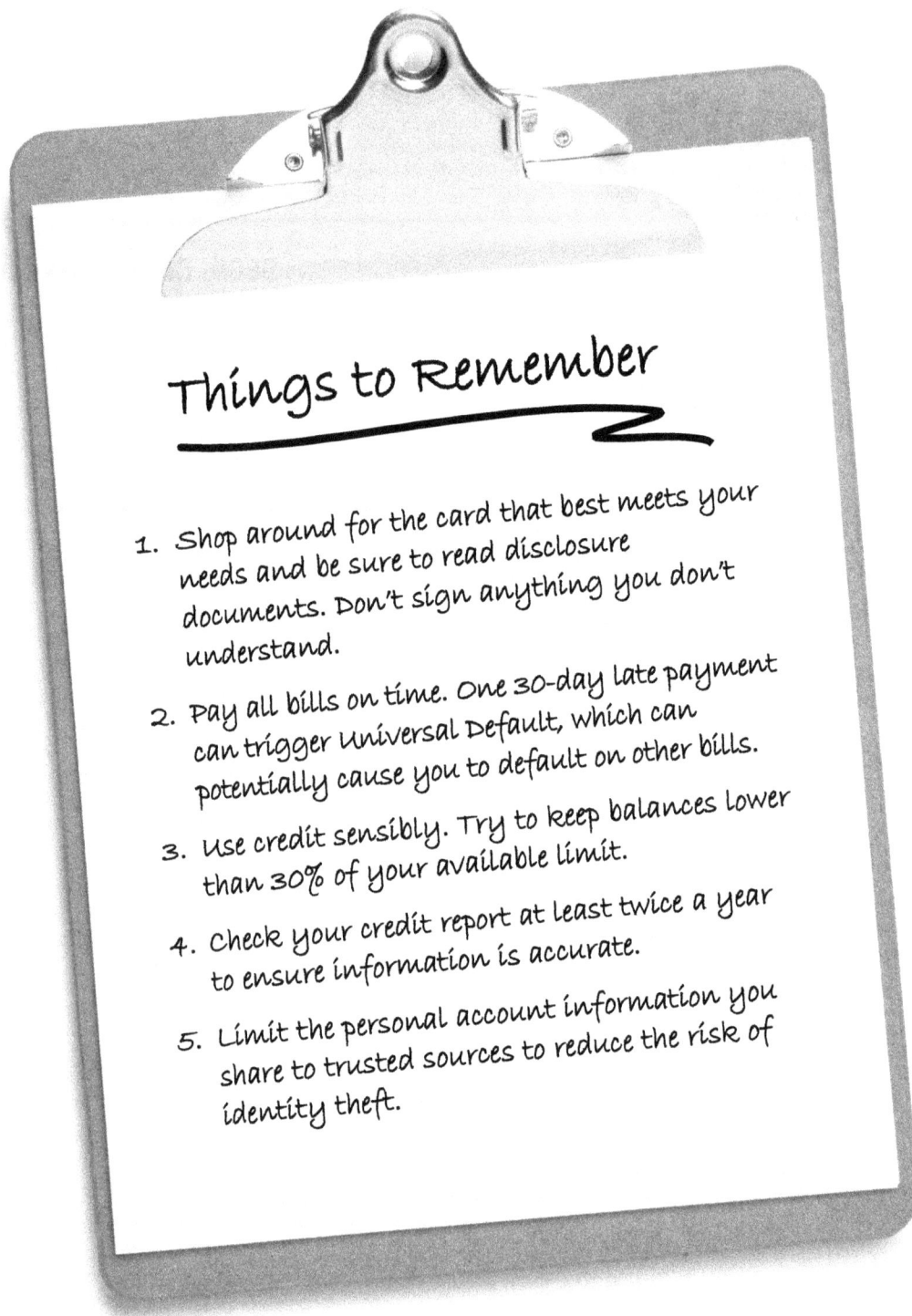

Things to Remember

1. Shop around for the card that best meets your needs and be sure to read disclosure documents. Don't sign anything you don't understand.

2. Pay all bills on time. One 30-day late payment can trigger Universal Default, which can potentially cause you to default on other bills.

3. Use credit sensibly. Try to keep balances lower than 30% of your available limit.

4. Check your credit report at least twice a year to ensure information is accurate.

5. Limit the personal account information you share to trusted sources to reduce the risk of identity theft.

END

END PART 2

PART 3

LESSON 6
STARTING A BUSINESS

OVERVIEW

Starting a business is a good way to achieve financial freedom. You are the boss; therefore, you have a major impact on whether the business succeeds or fails. It's also important to have a passion for the product or service you offer because when you are doing something you truly enjoy, it makes working fun and not a chore.

Questions to Ask Yourself Before Starting a Business:

1. Will you be able to acquire enough start-up capital to fund your business for at least the first year?

2. Do you have the passion and enthusiasm to sell your product or service to others?

3. Do you have friends or family that can provide advice in areas where you lack expertise?

4. Are you detail-oriented?

5. Have you done research to determine whether there is a large enough opportunity for you to earn a profit with your product or service?

6. Are you self-motivated?

7. Do you work well under pressure?

8. Are you willing to make the commitments necessary to grow your business?

If you answered "no" to any of the questions, go back and determine what it would take to change the answer to a "yes." Running a business requires a huge commitment and should not be taken lightly.

YOUR BUSINESS PLAN

Now that you have decided to start your own company, you will need a business plan. Just as a builder would use a blueprint to help construct a house, a business owner needs a guide to help grow a company.

Here are the components of a solid business plan:

➤ **Executive Summary** – This is the first section of your business plan, but it should be written last. Here, you, provide a brief summary of the business plan to grab the attention of lenders or investors. Make it shine. If people lose interest while reading your executive summary, many won't waste time reading the rest of your plan..

➤ **Company Overview** – This section provides information such as your company's goals. It would also include your mission statement, which is a brief description of why you are in business.

➤ **Product Overview** – This part is devoted to discussing your product or service. This is the area where you should highlight any unique features that will make it stand out from your competition.

➤ **Marketing Plan** – This is probably the most important section of your business plan. Before writing, do research to better understand your target market. This may involve conducting interviews to find out your audience's likes and dislikes. Also, research the competition to determine how your product compares. After this, figure out how you will market your product and how much will be spent on promotions and advertising.

➤ **Management** – This section should provide background on your firm's employees. Emphasize any certifications or licenses employees have earned that relate to the product or service you are offering. You may also want to include resumes of key personnel.

➤ **Operational Plan** – This part should cover how you will produce and deliver your product or service. Discuss the particular processes and costs to manufacture your product. You may also want to discuss any intellectual property, such as patents or copyrights, that are relevant.

➤ **Financial Projections** – This section can help you manage your business. You should project your sales and expenses for the next two to three years. Doing so will provide a measuring stick of how well your company is performing. Include a balance sheet, income statement and cash flow statement.

INCOME STATEMENT

Want to know whether your company is making or losing money? Then construct an income statement in which you list all sources of sales and subtract expenses from sales and enter on the bottom line of the chart. If the result is a positive number, it means the company made a profit; a negative number indicates a loss.

Sample Income Statement

	1ST QUARTER	2ND QUARTER	3RD QUARTER	4TH QUARTER	TOTAL
SALES	1000	1400	1650	1800	5850
EXPENSES					
Rent	500	500	500	500	2000
Payroll	700	700	700	700	2800
Marketing	100	0	100	0	200
Office Supplies	30	10	5	0	45
Telephone	30	30	30	30	120
Internet	15	15	15	15	60
Accounting	0	0	0	0	0
Legal	150	150	150	150	600
Taxes	60	60	60	60	240
Other					
Other					
TOTAL EXPENSES	1585	1465	1560	1455	6065
SALES - EXPENSES	-585	-65	90	345	-215

CASH FLOW STATEMENT

The cash flow statement measures a company's ability to pay its bills. A company with negative cash flow will have to resort to getting loans or investments to fund its operations.

Sample Cash Flow Statement

	1ST QUARTER	2ND QUARTER	3RD QUARTER	4TH QUARTER	TOTAL
BEGINNING CASH	2000	1415	-65	90	3440
CASH INFLOWS					
Sales	1000	1400	1650	1800	5850
Loans/ cash infusion				1000	1000
TOTAL CASH INFLOW	1000	1400	1650	2800	6850
CASH OUTFLOWS					
Rent	500	500	500	500	2000
Payroll	700	700	700	700	2800
Marketing	100	0	100	0	200
Office Supplies	30	10	5	0	45
Telephone	30	30	30	30	120
Internet	15	15	15	15	60
Accounting	0	0	0	0	0
Legal	150	150	150	150	600
Taxes	60	60	60	60	240
Other					
Other					
TOTAL CASH OUTFLOWS	1585	1465	1560	1455	6065
ENDING CASH	1415	-65	90	1345	

BALANCE SHEET

The balance sheet is used to summarize what a company owns (its assets), what it owes (its liabilities) and what shareholders own (shareholders' equity) at any given point in time. It's called a balance sheet because the total of the left side of the table below (Assets) must equal the right side (Liabilities + Shareholder's equity).

Sample Balance Sheet

ASSETS

Current Assets

Cash	1,345
Accounts receivable	
Inventory	
Short-term investments	3,000
Prepaid expenses	
Total Current Assets	**4,345**

Fixed Assets

Property	20,000
Equipment	12,000
Furniture and fixtures	1,000
Total Net Fixed Assets	**33,000**

TOTAL ASSETS	**37,345**

LIABILITIES

Current Liabilities

Accounts payable	1,415
Taxes payable	
Accrued payroll	2,800
Total Current Liabilities	**4,215**

Long-term Liabilities

Mortgage	18,000
Other long-term liabilities	11,000
Total Long-Term Liabilities	**29,000**

Shareholders' Equity

Capital stock	4,345
Retained earnings	-215
Total Shareholders' Equity	**4,130**

TOTAL LIABILITIES & EQUITY	**37,345**

THINGS TO DO BEFORE STARTING A BUSINESS

✔ **Product or Service** – Use your creativity to develop your product or service. It does not have to necessarily be cutting-edge technology. Maybe you want to offer a dry cleaning service, but to separate your company from all the others you decide to offer a pickup and drop-off service to make it convenient for busy individuals.

✔ **Market Potential** - Before spending too much money on your business, research the market potential. If there are several products available that perform the same service, you will need to think of a way to differentiate yours from the competition to give consumers a good reason to buy your product.

✔ **Advisors/Mentors** – Seek mentors in your field. They can be valuable resources for advice on running your business.

✔ **Start-up Costs** – Make a list of all the costs needed to operate your business. Include the cost of equipment, labor and any other overhead costs. Because many businesses are not profitable in the first year, save enough cash to pay your household and company expenses for the first 12 months.

✔ **Break-Even Point** – This is the level at which sales equal expenses. So you have no profit or loss. It's important to know how much money you need to generate to keep your business profitable and to manage its growth effectively. For example, if you plan to increase advertising costs, a break-even analysis will help you figure out how much your sales need to increase to cover the additional expenses. To determine the break-even point, you will need to know these three things:

Fixed Costs: These are costs you have every month that don't change, like rent or insurance.

Sales: This is the amount your business receives from selling a product.

Average Profit Per Sale: To calculate the profit for each sale, deduct the cost to produce the item from the price you charge customers. For example, if it costs $15 to make the product and you charge $25, then your profit per sale is $10 ($25-$15). With this information, then calculate the profit percentage by dividing the costs by the selling price to determine the profit percentage ($15/$25 = 60%).

To calculate your break-even point, divide fixed costs by the profit percentage. The business in our example has $1,000 in fixed costs each month, so it needs to sell 1,667 units ($1,000/0.6) every month to break even.

✔ **Business Structure** – The four main types of business structures are: Corporation, Partnership, Limited Liability Corporation and Sole Proprietor.

ENTITY	ADVANTAGE	DISADVANTAGE
Corporation	Limited liability. You can't lose more than your investment	Double taxation: Corporate profits and dividends to shareholders are taxed
Partnership	Easy to form. Single taxation: there are no corporate taxes. All profits and losses are reported on each partner's tax return	General partners have unlimited liability
Limited Liability Corporation (LLC)	Set up like a corporation to provide limited liability. Taxed like a partnership.	A lawyer may be required to set up an LLC, which can be expensive, depending on the structure.
Sole Proprietor	Cheapest and easiest to form	Unlimited liability. Your personal assets are at risk for lawsuits and no tax benefits

1. **Licenses or Permits** – You may need to obtain permits or licenses from your local government to sell certain products.

2. **Business Insurance** – Be sure to talk with an insurance agent about your business plans; he or she can help point out risks and recommend the appropriate type of insurance coverage needed to protect yourself in case of a loss or lawsuit. Also, don't forget about health care coverage. If you plan to quit a job where you had health insurance, consider using the Consolidated Omnibus Budget Reconciliation Act of 1985 (COBRA). This allows you to continue receiving health coverage after you leave your job for up to 18 months; however, you will have to pay the full cost of premiums. You can also research various insurance companies to find a program that best meets your medical needs.

3. **Business Plan** – There is no standard length for a business plan. It's possible that your plan may start out as five pages, but as your business grows and you pursue other market opportunities, it may become 50 pages or more.

4. **Record-keeping system** – It's a good idea to have a ledger or a software package like Quick Books to keep track of sales and expenses. Having your records in order will make life easier when it's time to file your business taxes.

ITEM	DATE COMPLETED

1. Determine product or service you will offer

2. Research market potential of product or service

3. Establish group of advisors/mentors

4. Tabulate business start-up costs

5. Determine break-even point

6. Decide on business structure

7. Check to see if any licenses or permits are needed

8. Consult insurance agent on business insurance needs

9. Develop business plan

10. Set up record-keeping system

TIPS FOR ENJOYING A SUCCESSFUL BUSINESS

➢ **Write Out Your Plans** – Put in writing the product or service you will offer to customers and how much you will charge. Also, make sure you have written agreements with suppliers and outside consultants that specify the expectations of each party and the payment terms.

➢ **Control Your Spending** – Because most businesses aren't profitable in the early years, keep a tight handle on spending. Don't make any frivolous purchases.

➢ **Keep Your Word** – If you say you are going to do something for a customer, stick to it. Be professional and courteous at all times. Treat customers as you wish to be treated.

➢ **Protect Your Assets** – Think carefully about the business structure for your company. A sole proprietorship is the easiest and cheapest to form, but it puts all of your personal assets at risk if you are ever sued. Consider a limited liability corporation or corporation in which only your investment in the entity is at risk, not all of your personal assets.

➢ **Love What You Do** – When you enjoy your business life, it makes coming to work so much easier. Find a business that you enjoy so much that you would be willing to do it for free.

Lesson 6 **QUIZ**

STOP

1. **Which of the following business structures provides limited liability?**
   a. Limited liability corporation
   b. Sole proprietor
   c. Corporation
   d. Both a & c

2. **True or False:** The marketing plan should be the last section written in a business plan.

3. **Which financial statement measures a company's ability to pay its bills?**

   a. Balance sheet
   b. Income statement
   c. Cash flow statement

4. **The point that sales equal expenses is called:**
   a. Break-even
   b. Profit
   c. Loss

5. **True or False:** A business plan must be at least 25 pages.

KEY

1. (d) Both a & c are business structures that provide business owners limited liability.
2. False. The executive summary is written last because it summarizes the business plan.
3. (c) Cash flow statement.
4. (a) Break-even is the point at which a company's sales equal its expenses.
5. False. There is no set length for business plans.

Sample Income Statement

	1ST QUARTER	2ND QUARTER	3RD QUARTER	4TH QUARTER	TOTAL
SALES					
EXPENSES					
Rent					
Payroll					
Marketing					
Office Supplies					
Telephone					
Internet					
Accounting					
Legal					
Taxes					
Other					
Other					
TOTAL EXPENSES					
SALES - EXPENSES					

Sample Cash Flow Statement

	1ST QUARTER	2ND QUARTER	3RD QUARTER	4TH QUARTER	TOTAL
BEGINNING CASH					
CASH INFLOWS					
Sales					
Loans/ cash infusion					
TOTAL CASH INFLOW					
CASH OUTFLOWS					
Rent					
Payroll					
Marketing					
Office Supplies					
Telephone					
Internet					
Accounting					
Legal					
Taxes					
Other					
Other					
TOTAL CASH OUTFLOWS					
ENDING CASH					

Sample Balance Sheet

ASSETS

Current Assets

Cash

Accounts receivable

Inventory

Short-term investments

Prepaid expenses

Total Current Assets

Fixed Assets

Property

Equipment

Furniture and fixtures

Total Net Fixed Assets

TOTAL ASSETS

LIABILITIES

Current Liabilities

Accounts payable

Taxes payable

Accrued payroll

Total Current Liabilities

Long-term Liabilities

Mortgage

Other long-term liabilities

Total Long-Term Liabilities

Shareholders' Equity

Capital stock

Retained earnings

Total Shareholders' Equity

TOTAL LIABILITIES & EQUITY

LESSON 7
EDUCATION

OVERVIEW

Education does not end after high school or college. You will keep learning new things for the rest of your life. In the workforce, some professions have continuing education requirements to maintain certifications or licenses. Receiving promotions may be dependent on you earning an advanced degree or completing certain courses related to your job. As the following chart indicates, people with a college degree have a higher average salary than those with a high-school diploma.

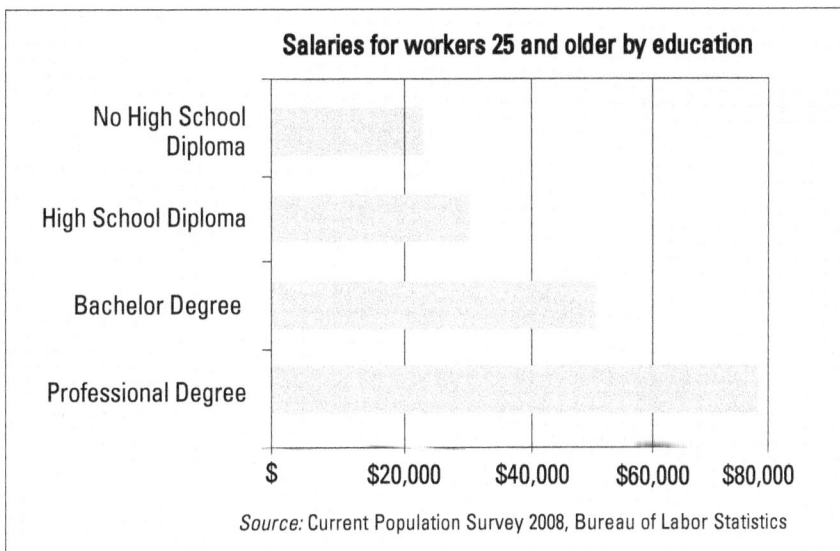

Salaries for workers 25 and older by education

	$	$20,000	$40,000	$60,000	$80,000
No High School Diploma					
High School Diploma					
Bachelor Degree					
Professional Degree					

Source: Current Population Survey 2008, Bureau of Labor Statistics

CHOICES

Continuing your education beyond high school doesn't mean you have to attend a four-year college. There are technical/trade schools where you can learn a specific trade. Community colleges can also help bridge the gap. These schools offer Associates' degrees, and many have programs with four-year institutions that will allow you to transfer credits that can cut down on the time it takes to earn a Bachelor's degree. If you are too busy to sit in a classroom, you may want to consider online colleges. These programs permit you to earn a degree in the comfort of your own home and on your time. Just make sure the college exists before sending any money. Do a little investigating to determine how long the school has been around, and remember — the longer, the better.

Also, try to contact professors at the school to make sure they are real people. There are so many "diploma mills" – supposed "schools" that allow you to "buy" a degree from a fictitious university. Below is an example of a letter from one of these "schools." Check out the Council for Higher Education Accreditation (www.chea.org) to find a list of accredited online colleges.

Home   Profile   People   Mail   Photos   More ▾

New   Delete   Junk   Mark as ▾   Move to ▾   🖨 POP

Reply   Reply all   Forward   ⬇ ⬆

High-Paying Jobs Require a Degree

From: **John Smith**
Sent: **Fri 11/20/2009 8:35 AM**
To: **info@PatrickALyons.com**

Virtually all high-paying jobs require a degree. If you don't have the degree you feel you deserve, or have a degree you feel no longer suits your chosen career path, let us help!

Simply call the number below (at no cost to you), and leave your contact info (your name and full phone number, and what time is most convenient for you for us to return your call), and we'll get back to you promptly with full information about the types of accredited degrees we offer, and the process required to obtain them.

Take a solid step to improve your life, and drastically improve your income!

*Call **877-Diploma Mill** for details.*

Reply   Reply all   Forward   Delete   POP   ⬇ ⬆

CHART FOR EVALUATING COLLEGES

School Evaluation

	SCHOOL 1	SCHOOL 2	SCHOOL 3
Tuition			
Room & Board			
Retention rate			
Alumnus interview			
Student interview			
Financial aid			
Resources			
Placement office			
Class size			
School visit			

Tuition According to Wikipedia.com, tuition means instruction, teaching, or a fee charged for educational instruction, especially at a formal institution. Private schools are generally more expensive than state schools. However, don't assume the quality of education at a public school is of lower quality. Lawmakers use state funds to subsidize the costs at these institutions to encourage local students to attend, which accounts for part of the price difference.

Room and Board includes the cost of renting a dormitory room on campus or apartment for living off campus and purchasing a meal plan. Below is a table comparing the costs of tuition and room & board for community college and four-year institutions for the 2008-2009 school year.

Retention Rate – This is the percentage of students who continue enrollment at a particular school. It lets you know how the current students feel about the school, so the higher the rate, the better.

Alumnus Interview – If an alumnus had a good experience at his school, he or she will be a great spokesperson on the benefits of attending that institution.

	TUITION & FEES	ROOM & BOARD	TOTAL
4 year private	$25,143	$8,898	$34,041
4 year public	$6,585	$7,748	$14,333
Community college	$2,372	*	*

Source: College Board   * sample too small for meaningful information

Student Interview – Talking to a current student can provide insight into how life is at the school you are planning to attend. If possible, try to find someone who has the same major as the one you will pursue to get an understanding of the requirements for the program and the amount of support faculty members provide.

Financial Aid – Since the cost of pursuing a college degree continues to rise, financial aid may have a major impact on your decision when choosing a school.

Resources – Resources can have a huge impact on your life at school. Check out the library on campus to see how extensive its book and periodical collection is. It's not uncommon to spend many hours in the library studying or doing research for projects, so make sure you have sufficient resources to do your job. Also check out the Student Affairs office to see what extracurricular activities are available. There may be groups or organizations on campus you want to join that share similar aims.

Placement Office – All schools do not have placement offices, so check to make sure yours does. Schedule a visit with the placement officer to find out what services are available. Workshop offerings such as resume writing and interview skills show that a placement office is committed to having its students prepared for life after graduation. Also inquire about internship opportunities. Internships can be a great way to try out a career to decide if it is one you wish to pursue. They also provide practical experience, which can lead to a job with the company you interned with after graduation, or give you an upper hand over the competition when applying for jobs.

Class Size – If receiving personal attention from professors is important to you, choosing a small school or a program where the class size is low makes a lot of sense.

School Visit – It's a good idea to make a list of schools you would like to attend and plan visits to each one. Try to meet with someone in the financial aid department to learn about what additional scholarships and grants may be available to you. Also meet with professors or academic advisors, if possible, to learn more about the courses required to earn your degree.

FINANCIAL AID

Now that you have made the decision to continue your education, you will need to find a way to cover the costs. Some people are fortunate enough to have a college fund stashed away to provide for educational costs, but if you don't, there are four options available: grants, scholarships, loans and getting a job.

Grants and scholarships are awards that don't have to be paid back. Grants and some scholarships are given on the basis of financial need.

Scholarships may be awarded on need or some type of merit criteria.

Loans, on the other hand, must be paid back, so exhaust all other resources before choosing this option. There are two types: subsidized and non-subsidized. Since subsidized loans are need-based, the Federal government picks up the tab for interest costs while you are enrolled in school at least part-time. Once you graduate, you are generally given 90 days to begin repaying the loan. Non-subsidized loans are not based on need, and the government does not pay the interest costs. So don't use these loans unless you have depleted all other resources, because they can be very expensive.

Each year, billions of dollars of scholarship money goes unclaimed. Students pass up several of these awards because they don't want to take the time to fill out an application or write an essay. However, you may get the award because you are the only one applying. Don't overlook small awards because the cost of attending post-secondary school is getting more expensive each year. Every little bit helps. Some sources to find information on scholarships include: the Internet, financial aid office, civic organizations, and churches.

NOTES

Lesson 7 **QUIZ**

STOP

1. **You can increase your earnings potential by attending:**
   a. Trade school
   b. Community College
   c. Four-year college
   d. All of the above

2. **True or False:** Diploma mills are legitimate schools that offer degrees for a minimal cost.

3. **Which type of school allows you to earn a degree by attending classes on the Internet?**
   a. Online school
   b. Diploma mills
   c. Neither a nor b

4. **True or False:** The college placement office is a source for finding out about internship and job opportunities.

5. **Which of the following is a source for financial aid opportunities?**
   a. Churches
   b. Civic organizations
   c. Internet
   d. All of the above

PART 3 REVIEW

Discussion Questions:

1. What are some benefits to owning a business?

2. How can continuing your education beyond high school benefit you personally and professionally?

ACTION ITEMS

	BEGIN DATE	COMPLETED
Make a list of advisors to approach to serve as mentors for assistance in starting a business.		☐
List schools you would like to attend or continuing education courses in which you would like to enroll		☐
List potential sources of funding to cover educational costs		☐

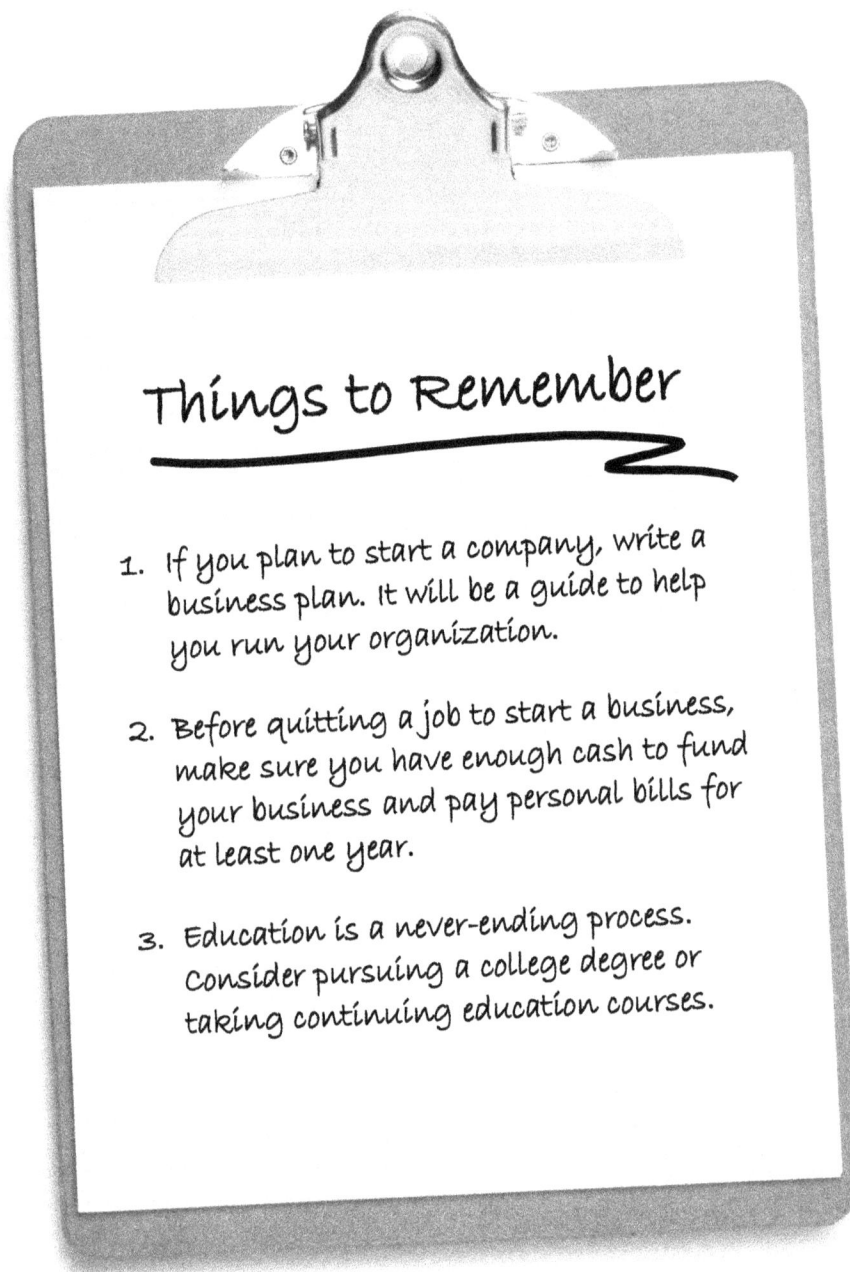

Things to Remember

1. If you plan to start a company, write a business plan. It will be a guide to help you run your organization.

2. Before quitting a job to start a business, make sure you have enough cash to fund your business and pay personal bills for at least one year.

3. Education is a never-ending process. Consider pursuing a college degree or taking continuing education courses.

END

END PART 3

PART 4

LESSON 8
RENTING AND BUYING

OVERVIEW

Deciding whether to buy or rent big-ticket items like cars and houses are major decisions. Take time to do research on the pros and cons of each scenario, because once you decide to leave the dealer with that shiny new car or sign the papers to close on that dream home, it can cost you dearly to get out of the transaction.

THINGS TO CONSIDER WHEN DECIDING TO BUY OR LEASE A NEW VEHICLE

What kind of vehicle do you want? Choosing the right vehicle takes a lot of work. After driving a gas-guzzling sport utility vehicle (SUV) for five years, I was looking for a mid-sized car that was more fuel-efficient than my SUV, scored high on safety marks and maintained a high resale value. These requirements narrowed my choices to a Toyota Camry and Honda Accord.

Everyone has different criteria to help with the decision-making process. After narrowing the list down, take a test ride in each to make sure it is comfortable. Choose carefully. Whether you are buying or leasing, it can cost you a huge sum of money to return a vehicle you purchased because cars lose their value every time they are started. Or, if leasing, you may face hefty early termination fees.

NAME	PRICE	COMFORT	WARRANTY	GAS MILEAGE	OVERALL RATING

How much can you afford? Try to make sure your car payment and insurance does not exceed 20% of your monthly take-home pay. You can decrease your monthly payments by making a bigger down payment.

| **Monthly Net Pay** | = | $2,500 | X | 20% | = | $500 |

WILL YOU BUY OR LEASE?

Buying gives you the most freedom. You can drive as many miles as you wish. You may make additions to the vehicle, such as installing stereo equipment or changing the paint job without worrying about violating a lease agreement. If you pay cash for the vehicle, you won't have to worry about making monthly payments and paying interest costs that go along with getting loans. This also allows you more freedom in choosing insurance options. Generally, vehicles that are financed or leased require higher insurance coverage.

Buying	
PROS	**CONS**
You own an asset	Higher monthly payments if you finance purchase
No mileage restrictions	Typically higher upfront costs than lease
Can usually get financing even with bad credit	Can have negative equity if financed over several years
Freedom to pay off loan early	Trying to sell can take a lot of time

Leasing a vehicle can be thought of as renting. The amount you are financing on a lease is the portion of time that you will use, generally three years. This is why monthly payments are cheaper than purchasing the same vehicle.

The good thing about leases is that at the end of the term, you can choose to buy the car at the price agreed upon at the beginning, walk away from the vehicle, or lease a new one. If your preference is to drive the latest car, then leasing may be a good option for you.

Leasing

PROS	CONS
Lower monthly payments	Mileage restrictions
Tax benefits if vehicle is used for business purposes	Leasing may be tough if you have bad credit
Always drive a late-model vehicle	You never own the vehicle
Don't have the hassle of selling the vehicle at end of lease	Vehicle must be in great shape at end of lease to avoid additional charges
Ability to drive a vehicle that you could not otherwise afford to purchase	Usually don't receive rebates

HOW WILL YOU PAY FOR THE VEHICLE?

If you will need financing, get a pre-approved loan from your bank before shopping for a new car. It helps speed up the car buying process and gives you leverage in negotiating the price, because the dealer knows you are a serious buyer. Having your own financing is also, in most cases, cheaper than using the dealer's arrangements for a loan. The dealer may be able to get you a loan if you have bad credit, but it will be at a cost - a high interest rate.

HOW MUCH WILL YOU PAY FOR THE VEHICLE?

Use the Internet to do your homework on what is a fair price to pay. Sites such as Edmunds (http://www.edmunds.com) and Kelley Blue Book (http://www.kbb.com) have calculators that can give you an estimate of a vehicle's worth. Several dealers offer Internet specials that allow you to buy vehicles for less than the manufacturer's suggested retail price (MSRP or sticker price). Always negotiate for a lower price. Haggle on the purchase price not your car payment. Dealers can get you a loan with the payment you are looking for, but they may finance the vehicle over seven or eight years, costing you a lot more in interest charges.

WHICH IS BEST?

Leasing or buying can both be good choices, but deciding which is the best option depends on your circumstances. If you like driving a new car and you don't drive more than 12,000 miles a year, then leasing makes a lot of sense. Also, your lease is likely to overlap with the manufacturer's warranty, which means major mechanical repairs will be covered. If the goal is to have an asset, then buying is the way to go. It will require higher upfront costs than leasing, but after you have made the last payment, the vehicle is yours.

Buy/Lease Comparison

	BUY	LEASE
Price	$20,000	$20,000
Down payment	$4,000	$4,000
Interest rate	7%	7%
Term	36 months	36 months
Monthly payment	$593	$312
Residual Value	N/A	$11,220

TO BUY OR RENT?

Paying rent or mortgage will be among the largest monthly expenses you will have each month. In general, you should spend no more than one-third of your gross pay on these costs. Below is a table that may help you decide which option is for you.

REASONS TO RENT	REASONS TO BUY
To avoid maintenance costs	To receive a tax break
To rebuild credit to buy at a later date	Fixed monthly payments
To avoid high upfront costs	Freedom to make changes to your home
Easier to move	An asset that will go up in value over time

SHOP FOR THE BEST LOAN

Before letting a lender check your credit report, shop around for the best rates. Call lenders or view current rates on websites. Also find out what the closing costs, miscellaneous fees to settle a real estate transaction, will be. They include things such as attorneys' fees, appraisals, and credit reports. See if any discount points are required for the interest rate you are quoted by lenders. Points are paid to lower your rate on your mortgage. One point represents 1% of the value of the loan. For example, one point on a $150,000 loan would equal $1,500. This fee would be added to your closing costs.

Lender Comparisons

NAME	APR	FIXED OR ADJUSTABLE RATE	CLOSING COSTS	PREPAYMENT PENALTY

GOOD FAITH ESTIMATE

When you apply for a loan, the lender is required by law to provide you a good faith estimate of fees due at closing. Closing costs can range from 2% - 5% of the loan amount, which is in addition to your down payment. You can lower your out-of-pocket expenses by negotiating for the seller to pay a portion of the costs. Another strategy is to get a loan with no discount points. The downside of this option is that you will have a higher interest rate on your mortgage. Below is a list of some closing costs you may encounter if you buy a home:

89

SAMPLE LIST OF CLOSING COSTS

	COST
Mortgage	
Discount Points	
Private Mortgage Insurance	
Appraisal	
Credit Report	
Prepaid Interest	
Origination Fee	
Home Inspection	
Insurance	
Homeowner's Insurance	
Title	
Title Insurance	
Recording Fees	
Other	
Attorneys' Fees	
Escrow	
Total	

GLOSSARY OF CLOSING COST TERMS

Appraisal – A qualified appraiser is hired to determine the value of the property. Banks require appraisals to help figure out how much to lend for a particular piece of property.

Attorneys' fees – This fee covers a lawyer's costs of preparing documents for closing and disbursing funds to complete the transaction.

Credit Report – A credit report is ordered by lenders to determine your credit worthiness.

Discount Points – This fee is paid to lower your rate on your mortgage.

Escrow – An account with a mortgage lender to pay homeowner's insurance and property taxes.

Home Inspection – Getting a home inspection is optional, but I strongly recommend it. If your inspector finds problems, you can request the seller fix them, reduce the price to account for the issue, or walk away from the transaction.

Homeowner's Insurance – Coverage to protect you in the event of theft or physical damage to your home.

Origination Fee – Fee for a lender to process a loan. The charge is expressed in points.

Prepaid Interest – Mortgage interest that is paid in advance.

Private Mortgage Insurance (PMI) – If your down payment is less than 20%, the lender will require you to carry private mortgage insurance for protection in case you default.

Recording Fees –Fees to have documents such as deeds and mortgage notes recorded with the local government.

Title Insurance – This insurance guarantees that the title is free from defects such as forged documents or unpaid taxes that would prevent a clear transfer to you. Title insurance protects you for as long as you own your home in the event someone comes forward and tries to claim ownership in your property.

TYPES OF LOANS

Fixed rate – The interest rate is fixed for the life of the loan. These loans are good for individuals who plan to live in their house for several years.

Adjustable – Borrowers looking for a lower monthly payment typically gravitate to adjustable rate mortgages (ARMs). These are loans in which the interest rate will change over the life of the loan. The rate will change every two years or some other predetermined time period outlined in your mortgage documents. Rates for ARMs are determined by adding a fixed amount (commonly referred to as a margin) to an index. Some examples of indexes used in computing values in these types of loans include: Treasury bill rate, London Inter Bank Offering Rate (LIBOR), Prime Rate, and Constant Maturity Treasury Index.

Interest Rate = Index + Margin

Example: You obtain a $150,000 adjustable rate mortgage where the rate is fixed for the first year and changes every 12 months thereafter.

ONE-YEAR ARM, $150,000 MORTGAGE				
DATE	**LIBOR**	**MARGIN**	**INTEREST RATE**	**MONTHLY PAYMENT**
July-06	2.50%	2.25%	4.75%	$782
July-07	4.00%	2.25%	6.25%	$924
July-08	5.50%	2.25%	7.75%	$1,075

From the table above, you can see that the mortgage payment increased 37% over two years. It's important to consider how changes in interest rates will affect your payments. No one can accurately predict the direction of interest rates, so think carefully before choosing an ARM. If you plan to sell your home before your rate can change, then this type of loan makes sense. There are some provisions in these loans to put caps on the number of times and amount your rate can be increased during the life of the loan. This protects borrowers. But as you can see from the example, rates can rise to the point that a home that was affordable in the beginning can become very expensive down the line.

FHA Loan – These mortgages are insured by the Federal Housing Administration (FHA) and allow borrowers to buy a home with down payments as low as 3% of the price of the house.

Interest Only – These loans are similar to adjustable rate mortgages since rates are fixed for a period of time and then fluctuate. However, you are only required to pay the interest on the loan, so the payment will be much less. The downside is if you borrow $150,000 and only pay interest for five years, you will still owe $150,000. This type of loan may be suitable if you plan to invest the difference between your interest-only and fully amortized payment in stocks or some other money-making vehicle. But don't use interest-only to buy a bigger house than you might otherwise be able to afford. Increases in interest rates can have a similar effect as the example of the 1-year ARM previously shown.

$150,000 MORTGAGE		
	INTEREST RATE	**MONTHLY PAYMENT**
5 Yr ARM	8%	$1,101
5 Yr Interest Only	8%	$1,000

IMPORTANCE OF CREDIT

Whether you are considering buying a car or house, you will need to make sure your credit is in order. Check your credit report for mistakes. Having low credit scores can cost you thousands of dollars, as the following tables indicate:

PAYMENTS ON A 30-YEAR FIXED MORTGAGE FOR $150,000

FICO SCORE	APR	MONTHLY PAYMENT
760-850	4.69%	$777
700-759	4.91%	$797
680-699	5.09%	$813
660-679	5.30%	$833
640-659	5.73%	$873
620-639	6.28%	$926

PAYMENTS ON A 48-MONTH NEW CAR LOAN FOR $20,000

FICO SCORE	APR	MONTHLY PAYMENT
720-850	6.05%	$470
690-719	7.65%	$485
660-689	9.63%	$504
620-659	13.36%	$540
590-619	18.11%	$589
500-589	18.72%	$595

PREDATORY LENDING

Predatory lending is a tactic by lenders to intentionally steer you to a product with higher costs than you might otherwise receive.

For example, a lender may offer Person 1 a 30-year fixed rate mortgage with a 5.5% APR, but offer you, even with the same income and credit scores, a 30-year loan charging 7%, which is also saddled with high fees. Minorities, women and elderly persons are most often the targets of these high-cost loans. Below are some signs of predatory lending from the Center for Responsible Lending:

1. **Excessive fees** – On competitive loans, fees less than 1% of the loan value are typical. On predatory loans, it's common for fees total more than 5%.

2. **Prepayment penalties** – In some cases, lenders charge a penalty in case you pay off the mortgage early. This tactic can trap borrowers in high interest rate loans to avoid paying the additional fee.

3. **Kickbacks to brokers** – It's not unusual to see a fee for "yield spread premium" on predatory loans. This is essentially a cash bonus a mortgage broker receives from the lender for steering clients into higher-interest loans. This should be noted on the Good Faith Estimate you receive from the broker.

4. **Loan flipping** – Lenders will encourage you to refinance a loan to generate fees for them even if there is no economic benefit to you. This can, in many cases, increase your monthly payments. Before you determine whether to refinance, get an estimate of the closing costs and divide it by the monthly savings. This number will tell you how long it will take to recoup the closing costs. Don't fall for offers to refinance unless the new rate will be at least 3% below your original rate; otherwise, the monthly savings may not outweigh the costs.

	EXAMPLE	YOUR COSTS
Total closing costs	$3,700	
Monthly savings	$250	
Months to recover closing costs	14.8	

5. **Unnecessary Products** – Occasionally, lenders will sell borrowers optional products, but may say they are required — which is false. An example is payment protection insurance, which will pay your mortgage in the event you are hospitalized or die. The fees can add thousands of dollars to the cost of your loan. Private mortgage insurance is required if your down payment is less than 20% of the loan amount; however, products such as permanent health or critical illness insurance are not required. It is illegal for lenders to extend a loan on the condition that optional products are purchased.

Lesson 8 **QUIZ**

1. True or False: Monthly payments are greater for leasing than purchasing a vehicle.

2. Which of the following is an advantage of buying a car?

  a. Annual mileage allowance

  b. Lower monthly payments than leasing

  c. The ability to pay off loan early

  d. None of the above

3. Which of the following is not a closing cost?

  a. Homeowner's insurance

  b. Down payment

  c. Attorneys' fees

  d. Appraisal fee

4. True or False: No maintenance costs is an advantage of buying a house.

5. Which of the following is a characteristic of predatory lending?

  a. Excessive fees

  b. Loan flipping

  c. Prepayment penalties

  d. All of the above

KEY

1. True. Monthly payments are lower for leases because you are only paying for a portion of the vehicle.

2. (c) If you finance your purchase, you have the ability to pay off the loan early.

3. (b) The down payment is not a closing cost.

4. False. No maintenance costs is an advantage of renting.

5. (d) All of the above are signs of a predatory lender.

LESSON 9
INVESTING

STOCKS

Stocks represent ownership in a company. Most stocks in the United States are traded on one of three major stock exchanges: New York Stock Exchange, American Stock Exchange or NASDAQ.

Stock Classifications

Stocks are often classified by size or capitalization. Below is a description of each category.

Small - Companies with market values less than $1 billion are considered small. Often, these companies are in the early stages of their existence and experience strong growth. The growth is unpredictable, which can cause stock price movements to be volatile, making these investments very risky.

Midcap stocks range between $1 billion to $10 billion in value. These companies can also produce rapid growth, but it tends to be more stable than small cap stocks.

Large - Large cap companies have values greater than $10 billion. There are several stocks in this category worth more than $100 billion, which are known as "mega caps" or "blue chips." Household names like McDonald's, WalMart, and AT&T fall in the large capitalization arena. These companies tend to have lower growth than small and mid-sized companies, but investors seek these stocks because they are perceived to be less risky.

HOW TO READ STOCK PAGES:

52-Week (1)							
HI	LO	STOCK (2)	TICKER (3)	DIV (4)	PE (5)	CLOSE (6)	CHG (7)
63.27	40.35	XYZ Corporation	XYZ	1.57	15	57.43	+0.43

(1) 52- Week HI & LO – This represents the highest and lowest price of the stock over the past year.

(2) Stock – Name of the company

(3) Ticker – A symbol that identifies a publicly traded company on a stock exchange.

(4) DIV – Represents the annual dividend, if any, the company pays. Dividends represent earnings that companies pay to shareholders.

(5) PE – Price/earnings ratio, which is calculated by dividing the price by the company's earnings per share for the past year. Earnings per share (EPS) is the amount of profits the company earned divided by the number of shares. For example, if a company has $1,000 in profits and shareholders own 1,000 shares of stock, the EPS equals $1 ($1,000/1,000).

(6) CLOSE – The price at which the stock closed at the end of the previous day.

(7) CHG – The change in the stock price from the previous day's closing price.

BONDS

Bonds represent debt issued by a corporation or government agency. These operate similar to loans since they must be repaid with interest. Most bonds consist of two parts: principal or face value, which is the dollar amount you are lending to the entity and interest. Bondholders typically receive interest payments twice a year until maturity, the date at which principal amount is returned.

Interest Rate = Index + Margin

Example: Say you buy a bond with a $1,000 face value that matures in 20 years and pays 6.5% interest. To calculate your interest payments, multiply the face value times the interest rate.

Interest Payment	=	Face Value	X	Interest Rate	=	**$65 annually or $32.50 every six months.**
		$1,000		6.5%		

Types of Bonds

Corporate – Corporations issue bonds to fund operations or make expansion plans. These bonds can be risky or safe investments, depending on its rating. Standard & Poors and Moody's rate bonds based on the company's ability to make interest payments and repay the principal at maturity. S&P's highest rating is AAA and the lowest is CC. Higher ratings are considered to be safer investments. Bonds rated BBB and below are considered junk. They generally offer higher interest rates than investment grade bonds, but there is greater risk the company may not have the cash to pay its bondholders principal and interest payments. Below is a table of the S&P Bond ratings:

Standard & Poors Ratings	
Rating	**Description**
AAA	Highest rating. Extremely Strong
AA	Very Strong
A	Strong
BBB	Good
BB	Marginal
B	Weak
CCC	Very Weak
CC	Extremely Weak

Treasury – These bonds are considered to be the safest because they are backed by the full faith and credit of the Federal Government.

Treasury Inflation Protected – One of the drawbacks of bonds is that the investment return does not keep up with the rate of inflation. You may pay $1,000 for a 30-year bond that pays a 4% interest rate, but if inflation is 4%, you are not making any money after adjusting for rising prices.

Real Rate of Return = Nominal Rate of Return (4%) − Inflation (4%) = 0%

In addition, at maturity you will receive $1,000 back; however, that will be worth less in the future because inflation reduces the value of your investment. To combat this problem, the Federal Government began issuing Treasury Inflation Protected Securities (TIPS). These are bonds where the principal balance is adjusted annually based on changes in the Consumer Price Index (CPI), an inflation benchmark used by the government. As inflation goes up, your principal balance rises. If we are in a deflationary environment, where prices are falling, your balance can't be adjusted lower than your initial investment.

Example: You just purchased a 20-year TIPS that pays 4%. The rate of inflation as measured by the CPI is 5%.

Principal Balance Adjustment	=	Principal Balance	X	CPI	=	**$50**	which would be added to the face value of your bond
		$1,000		5%			

Municipal – Bonds issued by a city or state government to fund things such as roads or government buildings. The stated interest rate is typically lower than other types of bonds, but interest is exempt from Federal taxes and the state the debt was issued, if you are a resident. Although interest rates are lower on municipals, you should convert the interest rate to essentially add back the taxes you would pay if the bond was not tax exempt to make a fair comparison.

Example: A 30-year corporate bond pays 5.5% interest and a comparable municipal bond pays 4.75%. You are in the 25% tax bracket.

Tax Equivalent Yield	=	Municipal Rate	÷	(1 - Tax Rate)	=	6.33%
		4.75%		(1-25%)		

Therefore, the municipal bond is the better choice because it pays 6.33% after converting it to a tax equivalent yield, versus the 5.5% corporate bond.

Commodities

Commodities are the raw materials used to make a lot of the everyday products we buy. Rising gas and coffee prices are just two examples of commodities we use on a daily basis. When the prices of these items rise, stocks and bonds typically fall. Therefore, you can protect your portfolio by having at least some exposure to commodities.

How to invest in Commodities

The simplest way to obtain commodity exposure for your portfolio is to buy exchange traded funds. When you are ready to sell, you can easily complete your transaction without the headache of finding a willing buyer. There are two types of ETFs to consider: Commodity-based and Stock-based commodity funds.

Commodity-based funds – These trusts are essentially mutual funds that make it possible for the average investor to participate in moves of the raw material. For instance, the price of gold on 7/28/06 was $647.80, but you could have participated in the price changes of gold by buying one share of the iShares Comex Gold Trust ETF for $63.21 on that same day.

Stock-based commodity funds – These are ETFs that consist of companies that prepare commodities for use by corporate and consumer customers. If you feel the price of oil is going higher, you may choose to buy stocks that produce oil instead of the actual commodity. Buying an ETF like the Select SPDR Energy would give you exposure to a basket of energy stocks. Stock-based commodity funds may not copy the performance of the raw material because companies may be involved in other businesses that are unrelated to their primary product.

SAMPLE LIST OF COMMODITY AND STOCK-BASED COMMODITY ETFs:

Commodity-based

NAME	TICKER
Deutsche Bank Commodity Index	DBC
iShares Comex Gold Trust	IAU
StreetTracks Gold Trust	GLD
iShares Silver Trust	SLV
United States Oil Fund	USO

Stock-based Commodity

NAME	TICKER
Market Vectors Gold Miners	GDX
Powershares Dynamic Oil Services	PXJ
SPDR Metals & Mining	XME
Vanguard Energy	VDE
iShares DJ Energy Sector	IYE
iShares GS Natural Resources	IGE
Select SPDR Energy	XLE

REAL ESTATE

Real estate is another area that should be considered when constructing a retirement portfolio. It can provide a steady stream of income if you choose to purchase rental properties. In addition, real estate prices historically rise at least 5% annually.

If you don't have a lot of money and want to get started in real estate, consider Real Estate Investment Trusts (REIT). You can think of them as real estate mutual funds. These portfolios can consist of commercial or residential properties. You can get exposure by buying just one share of the REIT. The advantage of REITs is that you can sell them just like you would any stock. You will have to pay your stockbroker a commission to sell, but it will be far cheaper than selling a piece of property with a real estate agent, who may charge 6% of the selling price as a fee. Below is a list of some REITs.

NAME	TICKER
StreetTracks DJ Wilshire REIT	RWR
iShares DJ US Real Estate Fund	IYR
iShares Cohen & Steers Realty	ICF
Equity Residential	EQR
Avalonbay Communities	AVB
Apartment Investment & Management	AIV

STOCK TEMPLATE

If you decide to buy individual stocks, write a one-page report to discuss why you like the company. Below are some things to consider in your report:

Description – It is important to have an understanding of the products or services the company offers.

Strengths – If it is a firm you feel is worthy of investing in, you should have no problem coming up with at least three reasons why it's a great company.

Weaknesses – There is no perfect stock, so be realistic in your analysis to pinpoint a couple of weaknesses. It is good to be aware of these points in case things don't go as planned when you buy the stock.

NOTES

XYZ CORPORATION

DESCRIPTION

XYZ Corporation is one of the largest consumer electronic retailers in the Southeast. The company offers installation services for home entertainment and computer-related products. XYZ Corporation is headquartered in Jacksonville, Florida, and has 312 stores in seven states. Last year, sales were up 25%.

STRENGTHS

Expansion Plans

I spoke with the manager of the store in my neighborhood, and he said the company is opening new stores throughout the East Coast. He further stated that the company's goal is to find stores in high-traffic strip malls where there are no other electronics stores.

Store Layout

I like the way the stores are laid out. When I walk in the door, there is a section with hot new items such as the latest gadgets, CDs and DVDs. In addition, all of the stores have the same floor plans, so I don't have to figure out where the computer equipment or game sections are located.

Customer Service

The staff is always friendly and courteous. The employees are very knowledgeable about the products in the store. When I have a product to return, they take it back with no hassles.

WEAKNESSES

Competition

There are other electronic companies in the area, such as Terrible Buys and Watermelon Computer, which have been around longer and have more locations.

Selection

Because the stores are about half the size of their major competitors, the selection is also not as extensive.

Activity

Choose a stock and write a 1-page report using the format outlined above. Track the price every week for three months and keep up with company news by using websites such as Yahoo Finance (http://finance.yahoo.com/) or MSN Moneycentral (http://moneycentral.msn.com/investor/home.asp). Use the table below to track your results. Has the stock worked out as planned?

STOCK TRACKING REPORT FOR XYZ CORPORATION

	STOCK PRICE	COMMENTS
Week 1	57.43	
Week 2	58.00	
Week 3	63.25	Earnings report was better than expected
Week 4	62.86	
Week 5	62.04	
Week 6	63.54	
Week 7	63.00	
Week 8	68.19	XYZ opened a new store in Washington, D.C.
Week 9	69.25	
Week 10	70.00	
Week 11	50.00	CEO fired because of fraud allegations
Week 12	49.65	

STOCK TRACKING REPORT

	STOCK PRICE	COMMENTS
Week 1		
Week 2		
Week 3		
Week 4		
Week 5		
Week 6		
Week 7		
Week 8		
Week 9		
Week 10		
Week 11		
Week 12		

ASSET ALLOCATION

Asset allocation is the process of spreading your investments among different areas, such as stocks, bonds, real estate and commodities to reduce risk.

Bond Percentage **=** Age

For example, if you are 25, you should hold 25% of your portfolio in bonds. The remaining 75% should be diversified among stocks, real estate investment trusts and commodities.

I recommend holding 10% of your portfolio in real estate investment trusts and commodities. These asset groups hold up better during high inflation periods than stocks or bonds, and can provide stability during turbulent times. The benefit of an age-based strategy is that while you are young and time is on your side, the majority of your money will be invested in stocks, which are riskier than bonds, but also typically earn higher returns. As you get older, more of your funds will be in bonds, which provide a steadier but less risky stream of income.

Below is a sample portfolio for a 25-year-old:

SUGGESTED ALLOCATION FOR 25-YEAR OLD

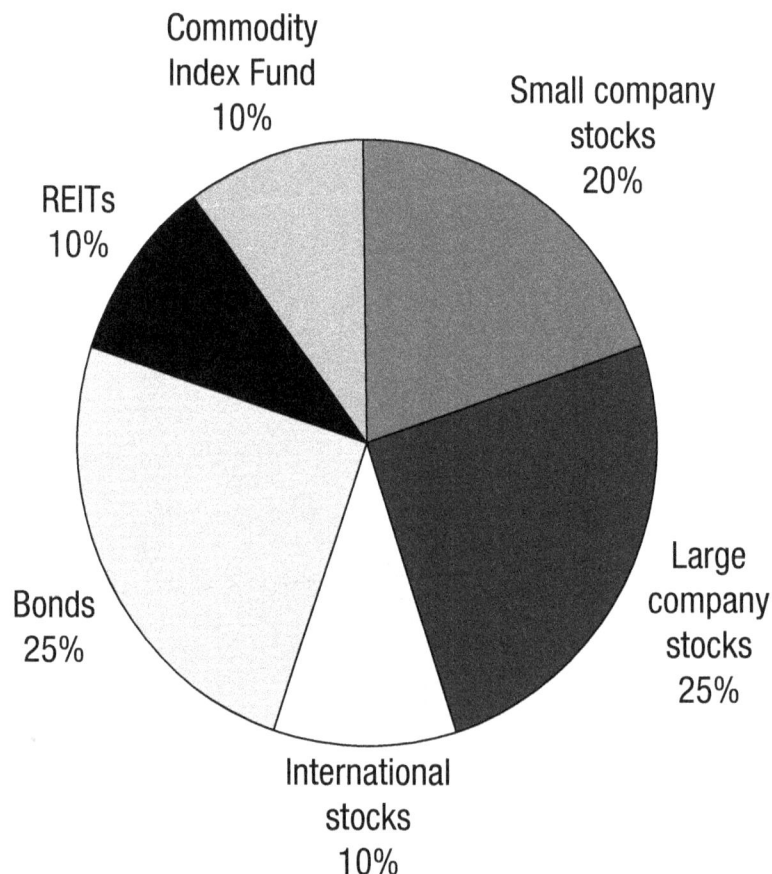

Commodity Index Fund 10%

Small company stocks 20%

REITs 10%

Bonds 25%

International stocks 10%

Large company stocks 25%

MUTUAL FUNDS

For the person who does not have time to choose individual stocks or bonds, mutual funds provide a convenient solution. Professional money managers construct diversified portfolios and monitor the investments on a daily basis.

Choosing a Good Mutual Fund

Fees – The expense ratio is the cost to run a mutual fund. Search for no-load funds that meet your objectives. No-load funds do not charge a sales commission. It's not uncommon for a load fund to charge 5% of your initial investment to pay its sales force. Be sure to know all costs involved in owning a mutual fund, because they can eat away your investment returns.

Returns – Examine past performance. Although it is no indicator of how things will fare in the future, you should look for funds that have consistent returns as opposed to those that post just one great year.

Portfolio Manager – Portfolio managers change firms occasionally, so periodically check to see how long the current one has managed the fund. Although you might have invested in Fund A, which had a solid five-year performance record, things may change if the portfolio manager leaves and someone else takes over.

Philosophy – Consider your risk tolerance level when choosing a fund. If you don't like risk, you should probably stay away from an aggressive growth fund and consider one that invests in stable, larger companies.

HOW TO READ MUTUAL FUND TABLES:

FUND (1)	NAV (2)	NET CHG (3)	YTD % CHG (4)
Lyons Mutual Fund	10.59	+0.17	5.60

(1) Name of mutual fund

(2) Net Asset Value (NAV) – The price to buy or sell one mutual fund share. The NAV is calculated by taking the value of the stocks or bonds in the fund and subtracting any liabilities, then dividing by the number of shares outstanding.

(3) NET CHG   The change in the NAV from the previous day.

(4) YTD CHG – The mutual fund's return from December 31 of the previous year to the present day.

Exchange Traded Funds (ETFs)

An exchange traded fund is a basket of securities designed to track an index. It could be a broad index, such as the Wilshire 5000, or a narrow one, like Leisure & Entertainment companies.

ETFs provide a great way for the everyday investor to create a diversified portfolio with a small amount of money. Buying one share of the S&P 500 SPDR gives you exposure to all 500 stocks in that index. Many mutual fund companies require a minimum balance to open an account, which can be as low as $500 or exceed $25,000.

Retirement Accounts

401(k)/403(b)

401(k) and 403(b) programs are employer-sponsored retirement plans that allow employees to save for retirement and receive a tax deduction. Many companies offer matching contributions, so it makes sense to participate – it's like receiving free money!

The table below shows how much an account can grow from age 20 to age 65 with a 3% employee and employer contributions for someone making $25,000 annually.

STARTING AGE	MONTHLY CONTRIBUTION	BALANCE AT 65 *
20	$63	$826,735
25	$63	$531,206
30	$63	$339,132

* Assumes 9% annual return

As you can see, large monthly contributions are not required to start accumulating wealth. A 3% contribution only costs you $63 per month, but you also receive another $63 from your employer; plus, you get a tax deduction for your deposits.

The table also highlights the fact that it is always best to take advantage of your youth by starting a savings plan early in your career. A 20-year-old who contributes 3% in a 401(k) account with an employer match could have amassed more than $800,000 at age 65 versus $339,132 for someone who starts in the same plan when he or she is 30.

Most of these accounts allow you to put aside up to $15,000 in a 401(k) account (as of 2006).

IRAs

Individual Retirement Accounts (IRAs) give investors more flexibility than 401(k) plans because it gives individuals the freedom to choose their own investment options, which can include individual stocks.

There are two main types of IRAs: Traditional and Roth. The table below covers the highlights of each:

	TRADITIONAL	ROTH
Who can contribute?	Anyone under 70 1/2 who has income	Single filers with income under $95,000 and married filing jointly under $150,000
How much can you contribute in 2006?	$5,000	$5,000
Deductible contributions	Single taxpayers with income under $50,000 and married couples filing a joint return making less than $75,000 in 2006	Not tax-deductible
Tax advantages	Earnings are not taxed until withdrawn	Earnings grow tax-free
Withdrawals	No penalty for withdrawals after age 59 1/2 and certain special situations. Others are taxed	Contributions are tax-free at any time; all withdrawals after five years are not taxed

NOTES

STOP

Lesson 9 **QUIZ**

1. Which of the following is a symbol to represent a company traded on a stock exchange?

   a. Dividend
   b. Ticker
   c. P/E
   d. Price

2. Which type of bond provides protection against inflation?

   a. Municipal
   b. Government
   c. Corporate
   d. TIPs

3. True or False: Asset Allocation means putting all of your money in one investment.

4. True or False: No-load funds charge a sales commission.

5. Contributions to a _____ are not tax-deductible.

   a. Roth IRA
   b. Traditional IRA
   c. 401(K) account

KEY

1. (B) Ticker is a symbol to represent a company traded on a stock exchange.

2. (D) Treasury inflation protected securities are designed to give bond investors returns above the rate of inflation.

3. False. Asset allocation means diversifying your money among several asset groups, such as stocks, bonds, real estate and commodities.

4. False. Load funds charge a commission

5. (A) Roth IRA contributions are not tax-deductible.

PART 4 REVIEW

Discussion Questions:

1. **What are some things to consider when deciding to buy or lease a vehicle?**

2. **How is the real estate market in your area? Talk with real estate agents in your area to get a pulse of the market in your zip code. Find out if prices rising and whether there is a large supply of houses on the market.**

3. **What are your saving goals (short, intermediate and long term)? Write them on paper and revisit periodically to see your progress.**

ACTION ITEMS

	BEGIN DATE	COMPLETED
Compare the costs of buying versus leasing your vehicle		☐
Set up a savings plan		☐
Open an IRA		☐
Monitor investments at least quarterly		☐

NOTES

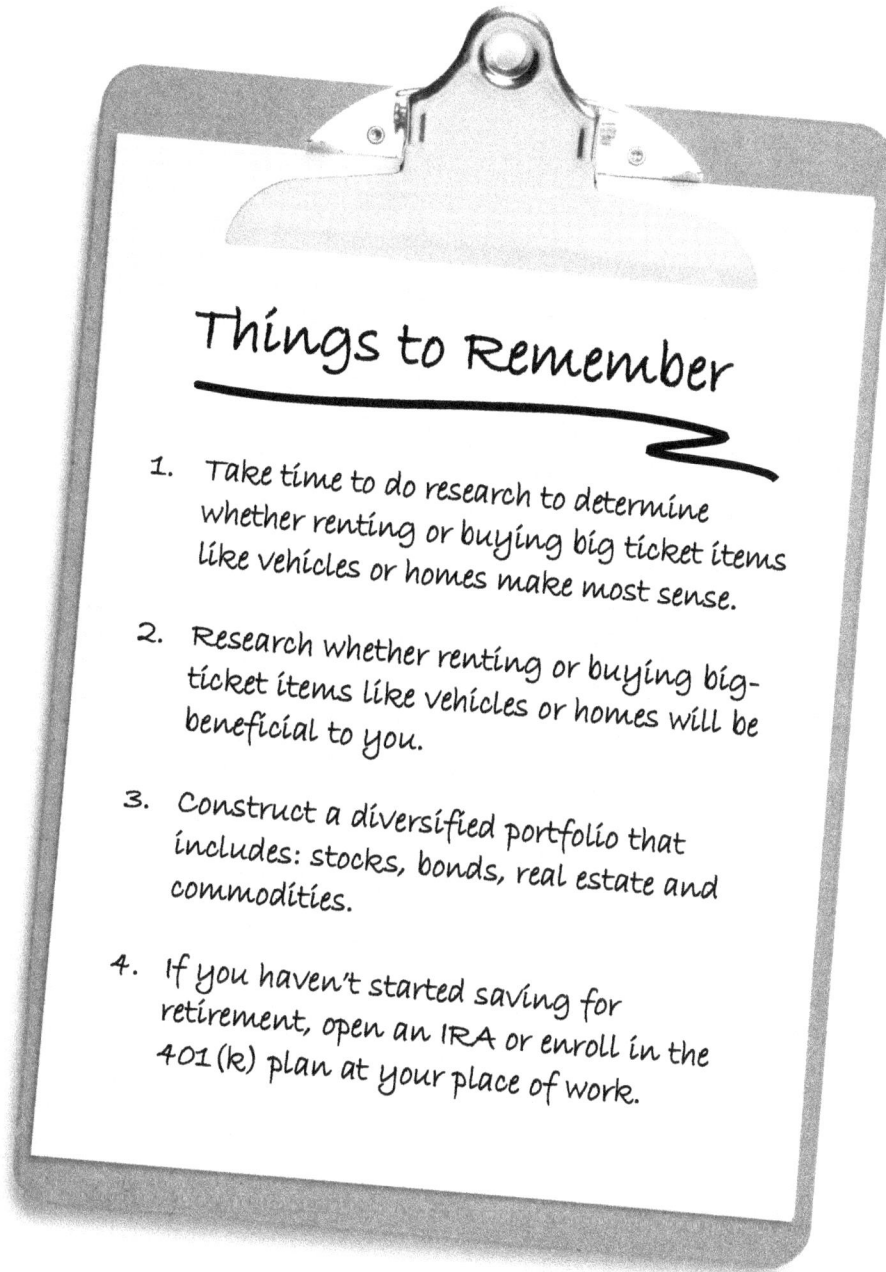

Things to Remember

1. Take time to do research to determine whether renting or buying big ticket items like vehicles or homes make most sense.

2. Research whether renting or buying big-ticket items like vehicles or homes will be beneficial to you.

3. Construct a diversified portfolio that includes: stocks, bonds, real estate and commodities.

4. If you haven't started saving for retirement, open an IRA or enroll in the 401(k) plan at your place of work.

END

END PART 4

EPILOGUE

Now that you have completed the last quiz and action item list, you are armed with all the tools to be a good guardian of your money. You understand the importance of using a budget as well as how to construct your own. You also have the tools to navigate the bumpy road of credit by having a better understanding of the fine print in credit card disclosure statements as well which types of offers to avoid. In addition, you have the knowledge to make informed decisions on big-ticket items like vehicles and houses. Lastly, you have the tools to construct an investment portfolio tailored to your specific needs.

I hope that I was able to accomplish the goal I noted in the introduction of making personal finance seem simple. It does require work to take charge of your finances, but I trust that you now have the equipment to become self-sufficient so that you can truly *Map Your Financial Freedom* with ease.

ABOUT THE AUTHOR

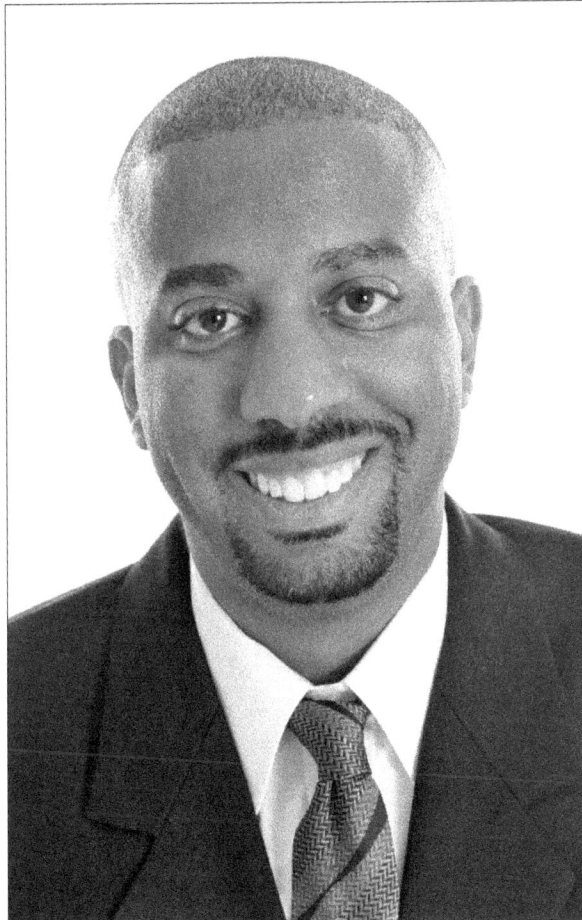

PATRICK LYONS

Patrick Lyons has more than 15 years of experience as an investment professional. Lyons earned a B.S. in Mathematics from Florida A&M University and an M.S. in Management (Finance Concentration) from North Carolina State University. He is the author of *Map Your Financial Future: Starting the Right Path in Your Teens and Twenties*. His investment and personal finance advice has been featured in the *Wall Street Transcript*, *The News & Observer* (Raleigh, NC), *Black Enterprise* magazine and various radio and television shows. Lyons has also taught business finance at Wake Technical Community College and conducted workshops on personal finance for several schools and organizations.

www.ingramcontent.com/pod-product-compliance
Lightning Source LLC
Chambersburg PA
CBHW051414200326
41520CB00023B/7225